# THE GHOST PHOTOGRAPHER

# THE GHOST PHOTOGRAPHER

*A Hollywood Executive's*
*True Story of Discovering the*
*Real World of Make-Believe*

## JULIE RIEGER

ENLIVEN BOOKS
—
ATRIA

New York   London   Toronto   Sydney   New Delhi

ENLIVEN
ATRIA

An Imprint of Simon & Schuster, Inc.
1230 Avenue of the Americas
New York, NY 10020

First Enliven Books/Atria Books hardcover edition October 2018

For information about special discounts for bulk purchases, please contact Simon & Schuster Special Sales at 1-866-506-1949 or business@simonandschuster.com.

The Simon & Schuster Speakers Bureau can bring authors to your live event. For more information or to book an event, contact the Simon & Schuster Speakers Bureau at 1-866-248-3049 or visit our website at www.simonspeakers.com.

Interior design by Dana Sloan

Manufactured in the United States of America

10  9  8  7  6  5  4  3  2  1

Library of Congress Cataloging-in-Publication Data
Names: Rieger, Julie, author.
Title: The ghost photographer : a Hollywood executive discovers the real world of make-believe / Julie Rieger.
Description: First Enliven Books hardcover edition. | New York : Enliven Books, 2018. | Includes bibliographical references.
Identifiers: LCCN 2018016449 (print) | LCCN 2018035439 (ebook) | ISBN 9781501158919 (eBook) | ISBN 9781501158896 (hardcover) | ISBN 9781501158902 (pbk.)
Subjects: LCSH: Rieger, Julie. | Parapsychology—Biography. | Occultism—Biography. | Ghosts.
Classification: LCC BF1027.R485 (ebook) | LCC BF1027.R485 A3  2018 (print) | DDC 130—dc23

LC record available at https://lccn.loc.gov/2018016449

ISBN 978-1-5011-5889-6
ISBN 978-1-5011-5891-9 (ebook)

This book is dedicated to my mom, Margaret Hadley. Here's the only way I know how to characterize this dedication: It's a love letter from a daughter to a mother.

Mom, I will never forget the day you said to me, "I knew exactly who you were the minute you were born." I'm pretty sure we have both always known that this wasn't our first lifetime together. You showed me unconditional love, effortlessly. I miss you being here. I miss your wit, your intelligence, your compassion, your love of Consumer Reports and Cat Fancy, and your unwavering love of Neil Diamond. I miss sitting across the table from you in full view of your refrigerator magnet that read: "A woman needs a man like a fish needs a bicycle."

You taught me to be kind; even when the other person didn't deserve it, you assured me that they needed it. The pain of losing you is so enormous that it can't possibly disappear entirely. The pain is just a part of me now, like an appendage.

What made you such an extraordinary mom is that you loved me for exactly who I am, for just existing on this planet. I can only hope we get to do this again. I would be your kid all over again, and again—for infinity.

# CONTENTS

# THE GHOST PHOTOGRAPHER

# Stumbling into the Cosmic Wilderness

*But once you have a belief system, everything
that comes in either gets ignored if it doesn't
fit the belief system or gets distorted enough so
that it can fit into the belief system. You gotta be
continually revising your map of the world.*

—ROBERT ANTON WILSON

*Freedom is what's left when the belief systems
deconstruct.*

—DANA GORE

**S**hit happens. We all have stories about events that changed
our lives, but it's the big ones—the life crises, the serious wake-up
calls—that fundamentally reconstruct who we are. Grief was the
dark alchemy that shook up my world. It blew open a door to the
Other Side—and yes, I *am* talking about ghosts, spirits, and etheric creatures that looked like they'd pranced right out of a movie.

People come into their psychic powers in different ways.
Some people are born with them. Others have to die first and

actually come back to life. And some folks develop psychic powers after they're literally struck by lightning. Well, ghost photography was the lightning rod that set my previous life ablaze, but thankfully I didn't get electrocuted in the process.

My transformation was not as dramatic as that, but it certainly was strange—*and* scary. I sometimes felt like I was at the summit of a giant roller coaster, looking down at the puny diorama of life on earth below and thinking: *Uh, excuse me? Can you get me the hell off this thing?*

Of course, there's no turning back.

If grief was the catalyst that kick-started my journey, ghost photography was the path that led me into the cosmic wilderness. I had the good fortune of finding an exquisite psychic Sherpa who guided me through this strange wonderland, though I didn't knowingly seek her out. And while there's no argument now that could ever convince me that the physical world is all there is, I'm still the least likely person to be into anything "alternative" or spiritually woo-woo. I may live in La-La Land, but I grew up in rural Oklahoma—and those roots go deep, my friends.

In fact, for most of my life I didn't even believe in ghosts. My family was not particularly religious or godly, either, though I was raised Episcopalian. (Episcopalians are the stepchildren of the Catholic Church.) I was also an acolyte, which meant that I walked down our church aisle wearing a white robe and carrying a cross. I had no idea why; my mom me told me to and I was an obedient kid. I think only boys were supposed to be acolytes back then; I had shaggy hair, and a few of the old churchgoing geezers actually thought that I *was* a boy. Talk about a real cross to bear.

I officially gave up on organized religion when I came out of the closet at age twenty-three. Christians didn't seem to be big fans of the gays, so I decided not to be a big fan of Christians. We didn't miss one another.

More important, my entire professional life is deeply rooted in the empirical world of hard numbers. I oversee the data strategy for a major motion picture studio and build data management programs that deliver insights into consumer behavior through data science, natural language processing, and analytics. I also manage complex media budgets with multiple zeros at the end of them. My official title is long and fancy: President, Chief Data Strategist, and Head of Media. (Essentially, I'm a nerd in the midst of some of the most creative people in the world.)

><~><

To say that my life didn't exactly turn out the way I thought it would is an understatement. (I think that's evident by the title of this book.) By all accounts I should be living in a big city in Oklahoma, married to my high school boyfriend with a few kids, and working somewhere cool like Krispy Kreme. (Okay, that's just a sugary fantasy. How about the *Tulsa World* newspaper?) I thought that by overcoming stuttering and a few other childhood dramas, my battles were over. I thought that I could live a normal and peaceful life.

That's not what happened.

I now lead a rather private—not to be confused with peaceful—life with Suzanne (my wife for more than twenty-five years) and our little furry children. My personality type doesn't lend itself to peaceful. I am constantly doing something. In fact, I've gotten up at least ten times while writing this paragraph alone. I always

have a project going on, whether it's sculpting metal, rock polish-
ing, throwing pottery, or doing something crafty. I once beaded a
wooden tissue-box cover for a friend. It was absolutely hideous,
but we all have to start somewhere.

><~~<

Everything in my life collapsed the day my mother died. Grief, by
the way, is like Baskin-Robbins: There are at least thirty-one fla-
vors. There's money grief, death grief, boyfriend grief, health grief,
divorce grief, sex grief, fat grief, empty-nester grief, got-fired grief,
presidential-election grief (I just added this one), and even something called Christmas grief (probably because you have to spend
time with all the people who participated in this list). Sadly, grief is
not a delicious concoction of milk and sugar churned together with
a delicious bag of Oreos. Grief makes you question why you're even
alive. Nothing matters, not even ice cream. You lose connections to
other people, then ultimately to yourself, which leads to isolation.
And isolation is not just abuse to the body; it's a jail sentence for the
soul. Ever wonder why solitary confinement is the harshest punish-
ment for our most hardened criminals?

But grief is also transformative, and it eventually catapulted
me on a journey. In *The Hero with a Thousand Faces*, mytholo-
gist Joseph Campbell wrote about the hero's journey, a narrative
that's become a major trope for self-awareness: A hero has to lose
himself before he "ventures forth from the world of common
day into the region of supernatural wonder," writes Campbell.
"Fabulous forces are there encountered and a decisive victory is
won: the hero comes back from this mysterious adventure with
the power to bestow boons on his fellow man."

The concept of the hero's journey has inspired millions of

people and was partly the inspiration for George Lucas's *Star Wars*, among other great tales.

My own journey was radical, transformative, and completely unexpected. That's why I was drawn to Cheryl Strayed's book *Wild: From Lost to Found on the Pacific Crest Trail*. Grieving the loss of her mother, Strayed hiked eleven hundred grueling miles solo across the Pacific Crest Trail to find herself. She effectively had to survive her journey in order to thrive in her life. In so doing, she changed her personal story and the story that women are told about their limitations and place in society. She grappled with her fears until she embraced her own power. "I knew that if I allowed fear to overtake me, my journey was doomed," she wrote. "Fear, to a great extent, is born of a story we tell ourselves, and so I chose to tell myself a different story from the one women are told. I decided I was safe. I was strong. I was brave. Nothing could vanquish me." You go, girl!

I was lost and found in a different wilderness than Cheryl Strayed's. Mine was a cosmic and spiritual wilderness that started with ghost photographs of disembodied spirits and fantastical creatures that sometimes looked like the very creatures in the movies I was marketing. In the course of finding myself, I found my sixth sense (and other senses that you'll learn about later in these pages). I was able to communicate with spirit guides, spirit animals, and deceased loved ones. I started using magical tools like pendulums, prayers, crystals, and sage. I fought dark spirits and started to believe in God after a long breakup. I can't turn metal into gold, but my journey through loss and grief was alchemical in its transformative power. In fact, virtually every aspect of my journey is alchemical in its transformative nature; some might even call it magical.

But like every roller coaster ride, the spirit world can be scary. I thought that I was a badass in real life, but I had to learn some hard lessons that even my spiritual tribe hadn't prepared me for. I had to work my way through some serious dark stuff to become a *real* badass in the face of the unknown.

Every single fiber of my body now understands that we humans have spiritual power over disembodied spirits precisely because we inhabit bodies. This is our true, essential power, and it can protect us if we learn to harness it. You are in charge of yourself. You call the shots, not some incorporeal ghost or dark spirit. Use this knowledge from the Other Side for the good of yourself and others on this *human* side—in this world, on this earth—and you are protected. That is the heart of the journey I'll share with you in these pages.

CHAPTER ONE

# Sangria

*Wild women are an unexplainable spark of life. They ooze freedom and seek awareness; they belong to nobody but themselves yet give a piece of who they are to everyone they meet. If you have met one, hold on to her; she'll allow you into her chaos but she'll also show you her magic.*

—NIKKI ROWE

I come from a long line of badass women. My grandmother was the first woman to manage a men's clothing store in Okmulgee, Oklahoma. Women didn't do that back then. While determining a customer's inseam, she'd shift their balls to the right or left without flinching. Odds are, hers were bigger than theirs. Ditto for my mom.

My mom, Margaret, was an accountant. She did bookkeeping for grocery stores, cattlemen, travel agencies, and oil guys in Oklahoma and Kansas. One cattleman never had cash to pay her, so he'd give her a side of beef or a whole pig. We had a Deepfreeze in the garage to house Mom's paycheck. The good ole barter system was alive and kicking in rural Oklahoma.

Margaret was also a serious badass who intimidated most men. This was in the seventies, when feminism was in the national spotlight for this first time. But the seventies in, say, California or New York, was more like the fifties in Oklahoma: Women were supposed to be happy homemakers who tended to the needs of their men. Margaret was *doing* the work of a man at the time: She was an accountant who decided to computerize on her own with an IBM TRS-80 computer, which back then was a little like figuring out how to build a Mars rover with a can opener in your garage.

One of my favorite stories about my mom dates from the mid-1970s, when she was attending an all-male state tax commission meeting in Bartlesville, Oklahoma. After the meeting they had a fancy sit-down gala dinner featuring a "special drink": sangria. (Anything other than beer and screw-top peach wine was "special" in Oklahoma back then.) All night long men would ask Margaret if she wanted a sangria, and all night she kept politely declining.

Finally, one guy asked her why she kept declining the drink. With a straight face she replied: "Because it makes my pussy twitch."

Every year thereafter, my mom was greeted with: "Hi, Margaret. Would you like a sangria?"

><

Bottom line: My mom never adapted to being a real southern woman. In fact, she didn't even try. She made the wrong food (no chicken-fried steak or Frito chili pie), wore the wrong clothes (no dresses, no frill, all-jeans-all-the-time), and had a foul mouth (the apple does not fall far).

To me, she was perfect. I was sixteen years old when she said, "I knew who you were the minute you were born." Even though my mom was not particularly spiritual, I know that in that moment she'd tapped into her higher self; it was her way of saying that she could see into my soul. I'm not sure if it was also her way of suggesting that we'd come into this life together for a reason, or that we'd probably experienced who knows how many lifetimes together (and would no doubt experience many more). God knows why we all ended up in Oklahoma in *this* lifetime.

But we *did* end up in Oklahoma, and my formative years will forever be part of that ravaged state.

><><><

Oklahoma is, no surprise, a zillion cultural light-years from LA. For starters, I don't blame the dust bowlers for coming here: Los Angeles on a shitty day is better than Tulsa on its greatest day. And it's filled with beautiful people, *literally*, especially waiters and waitresses. They're absolutely gorgeous, which makes me not want to go out to eat. That goes for people's pets, too, by the way. In Oklahoma, dogs fetch. In LA, dogs are fetching.

The state is famous for its college sports and its oil. It's not famous for diversity and tolerance. Its name comes from the Native American words "okla" and "humma," which means "red people." And that's because the state originally belonged to Native Americans until the Indian Appropriations Act of 1889, when Congress forced them off their ancestral homeland via what was called the "Trail of Tears." Years later those white folks deeded that same Indian land *back* to the Indians. Talk about a super shitty deal for the Indians.

Some pioneers (aka greedy-ass homesteaders) couldn't seize the land fast enough and staked their claims on the nicest chunks of land *before* the official launch of the Indian Appropriations Act.

Those folks were called "sooners," which became synonymous not only with the state's college football but also with anyone who snuck out in the middle of the night to claim their turf before the land rush.

I have no idea why the sooners were in such a hurry to get their land in Oklahoma; I couldn't wait to get out of that state. Oklahoma was founded by some very bad dudes who were not only stealing other people's land, they were stealing it before other potential thieves could get their hands on it. These real estate tycoons and developers raked in big bucks on the backs of the unsuspecting workers and laid the groundwork for today's fat-cat developers who are doing the exact same thing. They are *still* ravaging the shit out of Oklahoma, never mind the rest of the world. They're fracking for oil, robbing the school systems of financial support, inciting hatred through racism, and motivating people to turn to meth for money and escape. A tiny minority of morally depraved bullies is getting richer and richer doing all the wrong things, and they're certainly not spreading the wealth around.

But okay, I digress. The thing is, I still have Oklahoma in my blood. It formed me. And though I see it now for what it truly is, it was my paradise growing up. I loved (and still love) many of the people I grew up with. I knew virtually everyone in town, from the gas station owner (where we got S&H Green Stamps and bought a set of encyclopedias) and the janitors at the local B. F. Goodrich tire plant, to fast-food owners, county clerks, and the local police.

The town I grew up in was a mix of Caucasians and Native Americans, and nearly every white person had Native American blood. (We were an anomaly because we'd originally hailed from the East.) I recall only one Asian family who moved into town with two girls. Each one became a valedictorian and left the rest of us in the dust because we were a bunch of stupid white people who could not compete. (I say this with great respect to both Asians and stupid white people.) Some of my closest friends lived in a trailer park and we thought nothing of it. I wasn't even familiar with the term "trailer trash" at the time.

I also didn't understand the connection between experience and belief back then and I didn't know Wiccan from wicker. When Sting was singing "We are spirits in the material world," I had finally stopped bedwetting at the ripe old age of twelve. What the hell did I know about spirits in the material world? All I cared about was golf and riding my bike around undeveloped land in Oklahoma that's now filled with Walmarts. The closest I got to the spirit realm was freaking *out* over the movie *Carrie*. Otherwise, I was all *about* the material world, and that material world was all about Oklahoma.

*When Sting was singing "We are spirits in the material world," I had finally stopped bedwetting at the ripe old age of twelve. What the hell did I know about spirits in the material world?*

It was decidedly uncool to be gay everywhere in the world in the early 1990s, much less in Oklahoma. Telling anyone in my orbit back then scared the holy hell out of me; people were shunned, rejected, and physically or emotionally abused when they came out of the closet. Of all the people I didn't want to risk losing by revealing my "secret" (all those who thought I was "awesome," from my teachers to my relatives), my mom was on the top of the list.

I finally told her at the age of twenty-three in the lamest way possible: by phone. I was living in a dive in Dallas with my then-girlfriend, Suzanne (now my beloved wife), when I called my mom and just blurted out: "So, uh, Mom? I think I like women."

Silence. Finally she asked: "You 'think'?"

"Well, yeah," I replied. "I think I know I do."

"Have you tried it?" she boldly asked.

"Of course."

The line went silent. This was the moment, I figured, when I dashed all the dreams my mom ever had for me.

One week went by—not a word from her. Two weeks passed—nothing. Finally, the phone rang three weeks later.

"Hi, baby. I just got back from Judy Long's house," she said. "We had a long talk about you. I told her that you were a lesbian"—she pronounced it *less-be-in*—"and I admitted that I was having a hard time and that you weren't who I thought you were. Judy cut me off right then and said, 'Right, Margaret, she's better; she can be happy now.' And you know, honey? She was right. So, do you have a girlfriend?"

I just sighed and said, "Yes, I do, Mom, and you'll love her. Her name is Suzanne."

When Mom or I commit to something, we commit. In no time my mom had joined PFLAG (Parents and Friends of Lesbians and Gays). She started hiring only gay-owned businesses to work on projects. She even hired my gay high school algebra teacher and her partner to paint her house during the summer.

Margaret loved me unconditionally. In fact, her three favorite words were "I love you." It wasn't until way later in my life that I realized not every mother is as awesome as mine. She was a natural-born feminist, too, and liberally doled out motherly advice that only a woman of her generation could. "You know, baby," she'd say. "You don't ever have to rely on anyone. You can do anything a man can do, if not better. Don't feel like you ever have to get married. In fact, you don't have to have kids, either. You can shack up and adopt if you want."

How right she was. She was the light of my life, the hub of my wheel. She brought me into this world and then, unbelievably, she left it. And I do mean "unbelievably," because I never believed that my mother would ever go away, nor could I have anticipated the depths of my grief when she did. My mom was like air or gravity, an incredible force of nature that I took for granted as a constant.

So much for the guy who said: "The only constant is change."

# CHAPTER TWO

# Can't Remember Shit

> *We are all the pieces of what we remember.*
> *We hold in ourselves the hopes and fears of*
> *those who love us. As long as there is love and*
> *memory, there is no true loss.*
>
> —CASSANDRA CLARE

I hate to break it to you, but here's one thing that I can totally guarantee you: You're gonna die one day. And that's not all: You're going to lose at least one person you love. We all come in one door and go out another, and we never know when our day will come. If you're lucky enough—or if you pay attention to my story here—you might come to realize that death can sanctify life.

I didn't grasp this even by a thin hair, however, when it came to my own mom. It took me years to assimilate the fact that she would die one day. It just seemed . . . *impossible*. But my mom was human, and she died from Alzheimer's.

I was rising up the corporate ladder in my thirties in California while my mom was spinning down a dark rabbit hole with this unrelenting affliction. I'd started to notice during visits that little things were "off" with Margaret. She was becoming forgetful and easily aggravated, which was unusual for an unfussy person.

Still, I had no idea that I was actually witnessing the beginning of her end.

As her short-term memory continued to fail, my mom announced that she was coming down with CRS (Can't Remember Shit). If I could rename Alzheimer's, that's what I'd call it. Having a funny acronym for the disease that would eventually kill her was my mom's way of denying its existence. So it was no surprise that when the doctor first suggested that she might have Alzheimer's, she took one look at him and said: "Fuck you." Then she stomped out of his office. Still, there was no denying the slow ravage of this abysmal disease.

⚓

There are seven stages of Alzheimer's, in case you're wondering. The first stage is called "normal outward behavior." In short, there are no changes in behavior. Whoever identified these stages should have said that there are six stages of Alzheimer's, because what the hell is the point of the first stage being "normal"?

The second stage is called "very mild changes." That's self-explanatory: We're talking stuff like misplacing keys or forgetting a word. I think I've been in this stage since menopause. The third stage is called "mild decline": Good-bye, short-term memory. The fourth through seventh stages are a series of increasingly shitty degenerations, from "moderate," to "moderately severe," to "severe," to "very severe." Those last three stages might as well be called the Black Ice Period. *Slippery slope* doesn't even come close to describing that southerly descent.

My mom kept up the denial for years. Suzanne and I had to constantly manipulate her to get basic things done, like steal bills out of her office to make sure they got paid. When I told her that it was probably time to stop driving, she looked at me incredulously. "Why?" she asked.

"Well, you know, you've had some memory issues."

"No I haven't."

"Yes you have."

The next day, she drove her car to a dealership and bought herself a new one. That was my mother. "Bullheaded" is one word that comes to mind.

✕✦✕

In *A Prayer for Owen Meany*, John Irving writes:

> *When someone you love dies, you don't lose her all at once; you lose her in pieces over a long time—the way the mail stops coming, and her scent fades from the pillows and even from the clothes in her closet and drawers. Gradually, you accumulate the parts of her that are gone. Just when the day comes—when there's a particular missing part that overwhelms you with the feeling that she's gone, forever—there comes another day, and another specifically missing part.*

Irving wasn't describing Alzheimer's, but he might as well have been.

✕✦✕

You could fill a library with books written about how to find the right job or fix your marriage, or what to expect when you're expecting a baby (never mind the massive pile of books about how to raise that baby once it starts growing up). But back then there weren't many books about how to deal with a dying parent. There was no *How the Fuck to Stay Sane and Not Collapse with Grief When Your Parent Has Alzheimer's*. I was completely unprepared for this. All I retained from my reading at that time was this line that I'd read in a medical journal: "100 percent mortality rate."

For ten years I witnessed my mother die a slow death. By the time 2010 rolled along, I was emotionally vacant. I remember driving on the freeway with Suzanne one day when I turned to her and said: "The joke's on me." The joke was simple: I'd broken up not just with the church and organized religion, but with God. I had turned my back on God, so God had done the same to me.

> *The joke was simple: I'd broken up not just with the church and organized religion, but with God. I had turned my back on God, so God had done the same to me.*

Now, let's take a quick station break while I possibly piss some of you off. (Yes, I'm talking to some of you Christians.) We all have our interpretations of what "God" is—or isn't—based on our faith, religion, and upbringing. It's a loaded word, that's for sure. In her book *Help, Thanks, Wow*, writer Anne Lamott took a shot at defining what it means for those who find the word too "triggering or ludicrous a concept." How about we consider God, she helpfully suggested: "The Good, the force that is beyond our comprehension but that in our pain or supplication or relief we don't need to define or have proof of or any established contact with. Let's say it is what the Greeks called the 'Really Real,' what lies within us, beyond the scrim of our values, positions, convictions, and wounds. Or let's say it is a cry from deep within to Life or Love, with capital L's."

Lamott concludes that it doesn't really matter what we call this force. "I know some ironic believers who call God Howard, as in 'Our Father, who art in Heaven, Howard be thy name.'" She adds that a friend of hers refers to God as "Hairy thunderer or cosmic muffin."

I was most definitely crying "from deep within to Life or Love, with capital L's" as my mom was dying. I'd ignored the cosmic muffin for years, then realized that, *shit*, maybe I could use a little help. Inside I was asking, or maybe I was imploring: "Are you there, God? It's me, asking about Margaret." (Yeah, I loved Judy Blume, too.)

By 2011, I was back in Oklahoma and seriously grappling with these existential issues because my mom was in hospice. I would have rather eaten crushed glass than associate my mom with that word, but there was no denying it: She was heading through that thin veil between life and death.

I flew from California to Oklahoma one very shitty winter day to be by her bedside with her caretaker and my best friend, Cubby, whom I met when I was nine years old. Our mothers were the first to notice our connection when the two of us were practicing our short game on the putting green of our "country club" in Oklahoma. (Imagine a 1970s-style Sizzler steak house in the middle of a clean-cut field and you get the picture.)

"You know, I think those girls are going to be best friends their whole lives," Cubby's mom said. To which my mom replied: "I couldn't agree with you more."

We've since gone through every phase of life together, from

getting high the first time on Mexican dirt weed and RV camping in the Ozarks, to protecting each other against mean girls and
having kick fights behind the backstop of baseball fields. (Cubby
always won because she's all legs.) Many boyfriends later, we both
came out to each other at more or less the same time. (I had an
inkling about Cubby and her "girl pal" all along), then tormented
our mothers by suggesting that we'd been lovers since elementary
school. There were no secrets that we didn't share (that's still the
case) and no limits to what we'd do to help each other (ditto).
We've cried on each other's shoulders in love and pain and have
cracked up so hard we've peed in our pants. (Come on, I know
you've done it, too.)

⤜⤛

So of course Cubby was with me that day when my mom was at
home in hospice. Oklahoma was experiencing the worst snow-
storm in a century at the time: A state of emergency was declared
as roads were shut down and snow piled up to the rafters. We
lived on powdered doughnuts, Mountain Dew, and spray cheese.
That's what pain tastes like, in case you were wondering.

One sleepless night during that period I was lying next to my
mom in her bed playing her favorite Anne Murray song from my
childhood. She was also a big fan of Barry Manilow and Neil Diamond. To this day I love them all. At around 2:00 a.m., unable to
come to grips with the idea that the so-called Grim Reaper was
zeroing in on my mom, I got a call from my dear friend Mona.

⤜⤛

I'm going to make a wild assumption that you've probably had a
Mona in your life at some point. Mona is that person who bursts

into your life unexpectedly and changes it almost by accident (and sometimes precisely *because* of an accident, as you'll understand shortly).

Mona was blond, bubbly, and loved baubles. She had a red convertible that looked like something a high-priced hooker would drive. She wore Jane Fondaish workout gear and ripped clothes *way* before ripped clothes became a fashion statement, and she was very 1980s in her clothes and color palate: electric blue and radiant orchid. Pantone calls the colors of that decade "vibrant and saturated, reflecting prosperous times and an upbeat mood." That was Mona to a T.

An accomplished singer, pianist, life coach, and psychic, Mona was always the life of the party. Imagine an entertainer with a huge heart and a dash of schmaltz and that's Mona. Oh, and an added bonus: Mona was also a lesbian, which she embraced later in life.

When Suzanne and I moved to LA, we ended up living twelve houses down from her and her girlfriend. We met her haphazardly through her girlfriend, who saw Suzanne and me kissing each other good-bye in our driveway. Mona's girlfriend was jogging up the hill and stopped to gawk at us. You could almost hear her thinking out loud: *Oh goody! Two girls!* She told us that she and her girlfriend, Mona, lived up the street; how about we come over and hang out?

Suzanne and I didn't have any lesbian friends back then, which I guess made us bad lesbians. But once we met Mona we became fast friends.

>~~~<

So here's the deal with Mona: When she was twenty-five, she was almost killed by a serious magnesium deficiency. Lying in the hospital on the brink of death, she experienced an NDE. Before meeting Mona I thought that NDE stood for network data element. When I found out that it actually stands for "near-death experience," I figured it had something to do with choking on a ham sandwich and having to undergo the Heimlich maneuver.

In the 1960s and '70s, Swiss American psychiatrist Elisabeth Kübler-Ross was among the first to study near-death experiences— or what was then referred to as "out-of-body experiences." She wrote the hugely influential book *On Death and Dying*, and was the first to articulate what's now commonly referred to as "the five stages of grief." Raymond Moody, who wrote the bestseller *Life After Life*, was later credited with having popularized the term "near-death experience." His book documented one hundred people who experienced "clinical death," were revived, and went on to recount what happened in that zone between life and death. Tons of books have since been written and research studies conducted, including clinical studies in hospitals that tested the consciousness, memories, and awareness of people who were clinically dead in a state of cardiac arrest.

When Mona told Suzanne and me about her NDE, I was what we Oklahoma peeps like to call "shit-shocked." She described how, lying on the hospital bed, she rose out of her body. Looking down on it as she hovered above, she saw ribbons of liquid gold emanating into her head, which was hinged open like an oven door. Then she had a series of experiences whose characteristics have been recorded by nearly every culture all over the world and share the same traits. Here's what they are:

*    The distinct awareness of leaving one's physical body (in the case of clinical trials, lots of patients described exactly

what was said and done by medical professionals during resuscitation efforts).

* Feelings of intense peace and unconditional love.

* A rapid movement toward a powerful light, often through a passageway or a tunnel.

* Encountering spirits, mystical beings, "ghostly orbs," or deceased loved ones.

* Receiving knowledge about one's life and the nature of the universe.

* Approaching a border or a decision by oneself or spirits to return to one's body, often accompanied by a reluctance to return.

People on both sides of the scientific divide consider NDEs both a confirmation that human consciousness continues after death and a glimpse into the spirit realm where souls travel after death. Mona was unequivocally convinced of this. Like others, she was reluctant to return to her body during that experience, but was "told" by an energetic force that she had to go back. And when she finally did return to her body, she came back with uncanny "knowledge about life and the nature of the universe." She had intuitive psychic abilities that gave her insights into people's lives and their psychological makeup, without knowing those people. She was keyed into the wisdom of various world religions without having read about them; she could "see" and feel things before they happened.

Anita Moorjani is another woman who had a remarkable NDE, which she chronicled in her book *Dying to Be Me*. After she waged a four-year fight, her body was riddled with cancer when she finally "succumbed": Moorjani was clinically dead when she

had her NDE. Miraculously, within weeks of regaining consciousness, she was released from the hospital with no trace of cancer.
She went on to write her book about the experience and her
incredible insights about our physical *and* metaphysical world
(including the actual cause of her cancer) that she garnered during her NDE.

Moorjani also went on to frame the immensity of the unseen
world in which we all live during a TED talk. "Just imagine that
right now you're in a warehouse that's completely pitch-black,"
she said. "In your hand you hold a little flashlight . . . and with
that flashlight, you navigate your way through the dark." All that
we could see, Moorjani points out, would be whatever is illuminated by the flashlight beam; everything else would be in total
darkness. "But imagine that one day a big floodlight goes on,"
Moorjani continues, "and the whole warehouse is illuminated,
and you realize that this warehouse is huge. It's bigger than you
ever imagined it to be . . ." The warehouse is filled with countless
completely amazing and stupefying things—some things we've
never seen or imagined before; other things that we recognize,
for better or for worse. "Then imagine if the light goes back off
again, and you're back to one flashlight," Moorjani says. You're
again seeing the narrow view of whatever is illuminated by that
beam of light, but "at least you now know that there is so much
more that exists simultaneously and alongside the things that you
can't see."

Those words would later turn out to be almost prophetic in
my case, though I've never had an NDE. However, when I first
heard about the phenomenon from Mona, I wondered if NDEs
were an LA thing, like kale colonics and juice cleanses. I mean,
honestly: Is there something about LA that makes people get in

touch with their inner Shirley MacLaine (whom I love, by the way)? If you told someone in Oklahoma that you'd had a near-death experience, they'd probably tie you in a straitjacket and send you out of state.

Mona notwithstanding, my association with psychics then was still essentially zero. I'd drive right by those psychic shops that are all over LA without a glance on my way to the supermarket, usually for black licorice and tequila. I'd balance those out with Atkins bars and throw in Nicorette gum once in a while—cherry flavored, because it goes better with Diet Coke—and an orange Hostess cupcake if I was having a hard day. That's when I'd eat my feelings. (It's also why I'm not skinny. I have a lot of feelings to eat. By the way, an orange Hostess cupcake is a fruit. In fact, it's a citrus.)

I now have far more perspective and think LA is the perfect place to learn about mind-blowing experiences, because it's filled with more creative, psychic, intuitive, talented (and yeah, flaky, freaky, and flamboyant) people per capita than any other place on earth. Architect Frank Lloyd Wright once said: "Tip the world over on its side and everything loose will land in Los Angeles."

If that was his way of saying that people who've lost their marbles end up here, well, folks, bring on the marbles.

>><

Okay, so let's go back to that moment when I was lying next to my dying mom in Oklahoma, in that excruciating hospice environment at home filled with sadness and spray cheese. Suddenly my phone rang. Before I could barely whisper hello, Mona said on the other line: "Baby, get out of your mom's room. You're beginning to take on her breathing patterns."

"Okay," I said, and walked out of my mom's room. Wait—
*what?* Mona was in Los Angeles. She was calling me at 2:00 a.m.
local time and had no way of knowing that at that moment I was
sitting beside my mother.

But somehow, from fourteen hundred miles away, Mona
sensed that my mom was close to making her final exit as Margaret Hadley. Mona just *knew.* That was part of her gift—the gift
that came when she touched the underbelly of death. She intuited things before they happened, including the fact that her own
life would change dramatically when she turned fifty.

# CHAPTER THREE

# Fish without a Fin

*Grief does not change you, Hazel. It reveals you.*

—JOHN GREEN, *THE FAULT IN OUR STARS*

On February 10, 2011, my mom, Margaret Hadley, left this fish without a fin. I didn't exactly float to the top of the water, but I was certainly motionless for a while. Sadness, loss, guilt, and regret were all on a marquee over my heart. I wore them with every outfit, every day of the week for months to come. I hated myself because I didn't quit my job and move to Oklahoma. I didn't move my mom to California early enough, either. I did try, but it was too late; she wanted nothing to do with it.

I was in an emotional black hole when my mom died. How could I grieve the loss of this woman who'd loved me with every cell in her body and stop hating myself at the same time? I lived in limbo. Nothing made me happy. No one made me happy. I stopped answering the phone. I stopped listening to phone messages. I still can't bear to listen to voice mail, as it provokes a huge emotional reaction in me. I have PTSD from all the calls I got during Mom's illness; every time the phone rang, something was wrong.

Mona would come over to console me during those dark days: We'd snuggle on the couch and hold hands while we watched television. We didn't need to exchange words; her presence was a salve. I never thought I'd shrug off the cloak of grief.

Five months later we celebrated Mona's fiftieth birthday at a party in West Hollywood. At the entrance to the restaurant Mona and I hugged for what seemed like forever before I left, then we stood with our arms still wrapped around each another, talking. We exchanged our usual *I love you*s and smartass comments. (I suggested she get a bra with more support.) "Girl," I finally said during our embrace, "your guests are waiting for you to come back."

"I'm not done yet," she replied, still hugging me tight.

I wasn't done yet, either—and I'm still not done, because that was the last time I saw Mona. A few weeks later Mona was driving home from vacation late at night somewhere between Arizona and California with her girlfriend, her sister Pam, and her brother-in-law Steve. The car blew a tire, careened over an embankment, and crashed into a ravine. Everyone survived but Mona. She was killed on impact.

Mona turned fifty and somehow, for some reason, that was enough for her on this earthly plane. She had intuited that moment. She may not have known that she would leave this world in a fiery flash, but she certainly exited her life with the same dramatic flair with which she lived it.

I was beyond devastated when I found out about her death. I wanted to retract whatever belief in God I had—to the extent that I had *any* belief in God. But a strange thing happened later that same night: When I finally fell asleep after raging at the universe, Mona came to me in a lucid dream. Her presence was completely and totally palpable. She was *there*, hovering in front of me. Then she floated over to my bedside, kissed my forehead, and said very clearly: "Everything will be okay."

# CHAPTER FOUR

# Brenda the Good Witch

*Might I offer you some advice? Forget everything
you think you know.*

—BARON MORDO TO STEPHEN STRANGE,
*DOCTOR STRANGE*

Mona was right—everything *was* okay. She just wasn't
right, right then. After I grazed my way through grief on powdered doughnuts in Oklahoma, I graduated to Randy's Donuts
in LA. I was like Humpty fucking Dumpty in pieces, living the
reality of the sixteenth card—the Tower—in the tarot deck,
although I didn't know jack about tarot at the time.

Tarot cards have been used for centuries as a divination tool.
The standard deck has seventy-eight cards that represent arche-
types and spiritual metaphors with symbolic meaning in people's
lives. Here's what you need to know for now about the Tower: It
depicts a medieval-looking tower in flames with lightning bolts
striking from on high. People tumble or leap from the ramparts
in total desperation. Some cards depict the tower blown apart,
with people impaled on sunken turrets or pinned down by giant
dislodged bricks. It's not a pretty picture.

This is the card you usually get when things are collapsing
around you in order for new things to be built. Sometimes shit

31

has to hit the proverbial fan and things need to burn down to *force* you to create new structures in your life. (And let's face it: generally our asses need to be on fire before we make radical change in our lives.) The Tower card also suggests that you can't rebuild structures the same way they were before; you need to build new structures from the ground up on entirely new foundations. It's futile to try to create the life you had before a momentous event like the death of a loved one, and guess what? Your life is not *supposed* to be the same. Grief changes us practically on a molecular level.

> *The Tower card also suggests that you can't rebuild structures the same way they were before; you need to build new structures from the ground up on entirely new foundations. It's futile to try to create the life you had before a momentous event like the death of a loved one, and guess what? Your life is not supposed to be the same. Grief changes us practically on a molecular level.*

These structures I'm referring to aren't literal, of course. They relate to the foundation of your belief systems and values. They have to do with the way you think and live your life every day— on every level. They're about rebuilding relationships with people, with yourself, and with your purpose in life.

Mona's son JJ ended up living with Suzanne and me for around a year before he got back on his feet. Days after he moved in, weird stuff started happening around the house: The lights would go on and off, music from Suzanne's laptop would suddenly start playing (including, I shit you not, the Psychedelic Furs's "The Ghost in You"). Out of nowhere the bathroom heater would turn on. "That's Mona calling," Suzanne would say.

Around this time our wolf pack brother Reuben suggested we have a group reading by phone with Brenda, a psychic who lives in Cincinnati. She is one of Reuben's dearest friends, and he hoped that she might be able summon Mona from her astral lair.

*Who's Reuben?* you might ask.

Reuben is a juicy Latino who spreads his love around like jam; Jimmy is his husband, an equally adorable and loyal man who is more private with his emotions. Mona and Jimmy were friends growing up in Cincinnati. Jimmy eventually became a Catholic priest, then left the church because gays were not welcome there. (Pedophiles, yes; gays, no.) (I almost deleted that parenthetical comment about gays and the church but decided, what the hell, it's true.) (I really like parentheses, by the way.) Jimmy met Reuben, who worked at Procter & Gamble in Cincinnati. They fell in love and years later moved to LA.

Over the years, Jimmy lost track of Mona, only to learn that she lived two blocks away from him. Suzanne and I, as established earlier, lived on the same street as Mona and her girlfriend. Mona was possessive of her friends and didn't cultivate connections between them, partly because she was an attention hoarder who liked to keep her "people" to herself. (She had her "girls" and her "boys.") But clearly we were meant to be together in the same spiritual wolf pack, because in a town with a population of nearly four million and an area of 465 square miles, what are the odds of us all living within four hundred yards of one another? You do the math.

⌖

Okay, so back to Mona in her astral zone.

Suzanne and I first met Brenda at Jimmy and Reuben's house for dinner one night when she was visiting LA. Brenda is a gorgeous, part-Hispanic woman with shiny dark hair. She grew up in a Wisconsin town named Waukesha, which means "Healing Waters"—a term that pretty much describes the sea this woman swims in. When we first met I thought she was the daughter of a Mexican witch doctor. In fact, her dad grew up near Eagle Pass, Texas, and ended up in Wisconsin working as a migrant farm-worker. If there was anything witchy about him, it was his love of the bottle. That affliction developed in Brenda a finely honed sensitivity to people's vibrations and emotional nuances, which went hand in glove with the psychic gift she was born with.

I'd been crying for months when I met Brenda that night, my usual animated self snuffed out by grief. So I had no real grasp of the full impact of her wise words when she looked at me before I left Reuben's house that night and said: "It doesn't have to be this way. It doesn't have to be so hard." Only later would I learn that being of service to others is Brenda's holy grail on this earth, and that she's so super psychic she should've been wearing a cape with the letters "SP" sewn on the back.

A few weeks later, Suzanne and I were at Jimmy and Reuben's place, getting ready to put Brenda on speakerphone. Brenda had never done a group reading by phone before, and neither had I. I had no idea what to expect. What should I wear? Should we bring a snack? Eat beforehand? Do we bring an offering to the dead? Am I in trouble? What did I know?

But okay, if Mona's spirit was actually going to somehow communicate through Brenda, I was ready to hear from her. I missed her so much it hurt. I may still have been crying at work every day at this point. I was mourning the loss of both my mom and Mona; any freshman psych student could figure that one out, even one who'd missed half their classes and didn't buy the textbook.

We all settled down on stools around a speakerphone on the island in Reuben and Jimmy's kitchen. I was ready for whatever Brenda was going to throw at us. I wore my Mona catcher's mitt, catcher's mask, and kneepads. *Hit me, psychic lady*.

"Hi, guys," Brenda said.

"Hi," in unison from the group.

Brenda proceeded to ask us to bow our heads in prayer, and I began to sob. What was happening to me? I was crying at the opening prayer. That's like crying at movie trailers. *Breathe*, I told myself. Just *breathe*.

Once the prayer was over, I got a grip. It was Mona time—*not*.

"Reuben, I have your mom and dad here," Brenda said. "We'll get to them later."

"Okay," Reuben said.

Brenda somehow asked Reuben's parents to step aside. Then she said: "Julie?" I thought: *Julie? Did she just say Julie?* Why would you say my name, psychic lady?

"Your mom and dad are here," she continued. Oh shit. *What?* My mom *and* dad? I didn't see this coming. My heart fell.

My parents divorced when I was just a kid; my dad died eight years later. Both of my parents weren't particularly spiritual or metaphysically inclined. My mom used to say: "When you're dead, you're dead." I wasn't even sure if she really believed in God, as in some bearded guy sitting on a throne in heaven, despite our churchgoing ways. And my dad was a Christian Scientist, a secret he kept to himself for some reason that will always baffle me.

Now here they both were, presumably fresh from a supernatural marriage therapy session, coming back together through Brenda.

"Okay, thank you," was all I could think to say to Brenda.

Brenda then told us she would bring Mona into the reading and would get back to our parents later. I held my breath as she started to "talk" to Mona.

Mona was a Chatty Cathy while she was alive, and she was no different in spirit form. Even though we heard Brenda's velvety sweet voice, Mona's words were definitely being spoken; her thoughts came right from her heart. Through Brenda she told us how important we were to her: We were always her first call. We were the ones who came to her rescue when she needed rescuing, who gave her love when that was all she wanted. She made us laugh at her keen ability to keep us apart for all those years, but told us that it was time for the boys and girls to come together. She thanked us for caring for her son (and I immediately thought: *So that* was *her fiddling with our electricity and our electronics*). She gave us advice on how to help him manage his grief.

Through Brenda, we told her how much we loved her, but after about forty-five minutes, Mona left. I guess she left to go party in the spirit world or visit Saturn or do whatever the fuck dead people do.

Brenda then brought in a few other spirits: Reuben's folks, whom she knew; Suzanne's grandmother; and, later, Suzanne's adoptive dad. Once he left, my torturous path to freedom began.

"Julie, I have your dad here," Brenda said.

I looked around the room, then back at the speakerphone. Almost thirty years had passed since he died. I was stupefied even to hear his name. He wasn't much of a dad in life when I was growing up, so that became my refrain: *I grew up without a father.* I played that tape over and over again, sweeping whatever daddy issues I might have had under the carpet. And though many will tell you that whatever you sweep under the emotional carpet often comes back to haunt you, no one tells you these things might come back in spirit form to *actually* haunt you.

I looked around the room one last time, trying not to lose it. *Dad?* I thought. *Ghost Dad? Is that you out there?*

><~~><

My father, Thomas Locke Rieger, was a nice-looking military man who was a beat away from being a colonel when he and my mom got married. He was respectable and honorable. He served in Korea and Vietnam and served his country for decades. His mother, my grandmother, was a bona fide member of the Daughters of the American Revolution, an organization run by women whose family lineage goes back to the nation's fight for independence from England. Service to this country is practically in my family's DNA. But all I knew about what my dad did in the military when I was growing up was that he was in "transportation." Those military guys kept tight-lipped about their assignments.

Mom claimed that his drinking drove her to leave him in 1974. Vodka was not his friend, though he thought differently.

Sometime after retiring from the military, he skidded off the rails, moved to Salt Lake City, and took a nosedive into the bottle. I do remember his drinking. I once saw him pour from a gallon jug of vodka that he'd stashed under the kitchen sink. Another time he acted like he was only drinking sparkling grape juice while he taught us a card game called Follow the Whore. He rode a bus to Oklahoma to visit us when I was nine or ten and we hung out together in the Elks Lodge, playing bingo while he drank. You could cut the smoky air of sadness with a knife.

We weren't close, that's for sure. He loved my brother and me—that I know; he was always excited to see us. But he also seemed despondent because he knew it was temporary.

Perhaps my dad should have stayed in the military, where he'd served his entire adult life; he became aimless and drifted when he retired. The military world is ordered and highly structured; the civilian world, on the other hand, is messy and challenging. He was a good man who didn't know how to operate in the chaotic real world. Alcohol became the salve for his frustrations and lack of purpose after the military. After all, isn't any form of substance abuse all about masking the pain of living? In my dad's case, it literally took the life out of him.

><~>≺

He was buried in Arlington National Cemetery. We didn't attend his burial, though. To this day I don't know why. I missed the twenty-one-gun salute; the soldiers folding his flag and handing it over to me, his youngest. Not a single human being with the last name of Rieger, besides his children, attended his funeral in Salt Lake City. They could have shown up.

I learned that day: Show the fuck up. Always show up. If your friend breaks up with their boyfriend or girlfriend, show up. If someone needs a friend, show up. If someone in your family dies, show up.

*I learned that day: Show the fuck up. Always show up. If your friend breaks up with their boyfriend or girlfriend, show up. If someone needs a friend, show up. If someone in your family dies, show up.*

"Wow, your dad is a big spirit," Brenda said through the speakerphone. "He's a powerful guy, Julie. And he says he's always been with you in your dreams. He wants to know if you remember dreaming about him when you were younger."

"I don't," I replied, though my head was reeling: *Did* I dream about him? Was he somehow present in the twilight zone of my sleep?

"Well, there *is* something he wants to clear up with you," she continued. "He says that he would like you to stop telling people that you grew up without a father."

Hold *on*. Tires screeched to a stop in my head. Those particular words spoke of something deeply woven into the fabric of my personal narrative. I looked over at Suzanne, who looked back at me with total acknowledgment because *she's* the one who knows: How many times had she heard me say that I grew up without a father? That tape went way, way back. Now here was my spirit dad on the Other Side, calling bullshit on me while Brenda communicated for him through the phone two thousand miles away.

"He says that he's always been with you," she continued. "Every time you won a golf tournament, he was there. Just ask for him, Julie. He'll be there whenever you need him."

And that's when I lost it. I absolutely lost it. Not only was I grieving the loss of my mom and my friend Mona, I was experiencing delayed grief for my father. It was a trifecta.

There was silence on the other end of the phone.

Finally Brenda spoke: "Sorry, guys, I have Julie's mom here and I can't communicate if I'm emotional." Oh great, my mom was making the queen of psychics cry; nice work. What exactly was she going to do to me? Honest to God, I didn't think I could take what was going to happen—whatever that was.

"Your mom is saying, 'If there had been a magazine on how to raise a gifted child, I would have read it.'" Okay, now I *knew* for sure that Mom was there. She was a magazine hoarder with a particular yen for *Consumer Reports* and *Cat Fancy*. She'd kept every copy since 1976. I lost it again.

"'From the very beginning, you made your way around like you didn't need any help,'" Brenda continued, speaking my mom's words. "'I wish I would have known more what to do to help you, but you were so gifted. You may look like me. You may act like me and talk like me. But that heart of yours is yours. You had to do things for a mother that no daughter should have to do.'" Then, after a pause, "'And I *was* nice to your father.'"

*And I* was *nice to your father*.

Those were the last words I spoke to my mom: *Be nice to Dad*. I have no idea why and had forgotten about them until that very moment. When my mom was dying, did I unconsciously intuit the moment she and my dad would reunite as ghosts? Did my mom finally do what I'd asked her to do for the first time ever (because she sure as hell didn't do what I asked her to do when she was alive)? More to the point: How the fuck was Brenda able to do this, whatever "this" was?

<center>~~~</center>

That first reading with Brenda changed my life forever. The specificity and nuance of the information communicated simply blew me away. There was now absolutely no question in my mind that loved ones had crossed over to the Other Side and reached out to communicate. In receiving their communication, I, too, crossed a threshold: In that moment I believed in life after death. It's that simple. In fact, I didn't just believe, I *knew*. And now I wanted to know more, way more. I wanted to know what my mom and Mona were doing outside their bodies.

*There was now absolutely no question in my mind that loved ones had crossed over to the Other Side and reached out to communicate. In receiving their communication, I, too, crossed a threshold: In that moment I believed in life after death.*

# CHAPTER FIVE

# Paranormal CliffsNotes

*Paranormal events are just edges of the infinite we "happen" to encounter.*

—C. DOUGLAS DILLON

*All a skeptic is is someone who hasn't had an experience yet.*

—JASON HAWES

We human beings like to dispute what others would call facts when they don't line up with the truths we tell ourselves. That's especially the case when it comes to invisible shit. But come on: Empires have risen and fallen partly based on religious differences, right? Well, religion is also invisible and faith based, but no one will deny the massive influence it's had over us for a gazillion years.

I'm going to talk a lot about the unseen world throughout this book, but for now I'll just start with a brief primer. First off, nobody knows precisely what ghosts are or why human beings have perceived them for eons. It wasn't until fairly recently, like around the Industrial Revolution in the late nineteenth century, that science and technology started explaining away unsolved mystical or supernatural mysteries as "psychological." (No surprise: traditional psychology and psychiatry also appeared around the same time.)

Before that you'd basically get burned at the stake for ghostly shit or anything that smacked of the supernatural, not because people didn't believe in the spirit world, but because they totally *did*: Remember, our country was settled by religious refugees (some might call them fanatics or extremists; just sayin') who had a keen sense *and* extreme fear of the supernatural. The Salem witch trials in the 1600s drive that point home. Wikipedia calls them a "vivid cautionary tale about the dangers of isolationism, religious extremism, false accusations, and lapses in due process." You could say the same thing about Joan of Arc: She led her country into battle and would be canonized as a saint, but that didn't stop the English from burning her at the stake because she heard the voices of Saint Michael, Saint Margaret, and Saint Catherine.

Six centuries and probably six hundred wars later, we're still doing the same thing: While science is trying to explain away the supernatural (mostly dismissed as hallucinatory), mysticism, spirituality, and the supernatural have become hugely popular—and pop culture can't get enough of it.

It's impossible in these pages to cover the huge amount of books, TV shows, and movies that have been produced about ghosts and the paranormal, from the dawn of cinema to the recent *Doctor Strange*, featuring Benedict Cumberbatch in his hotshit red cape. The paranormal film genre is now one of the most popular genres of all time. Mediums have also become mainstream and massively popular, from John Edward and Concetta Bertoldi to Theresa Caputo and James Van Praagh, to name just a few. (I'll get to some of them later.) The bottom line: Paranormal films are *the* most profitable genre in the business.

Consider these stats:

* Every two seconds, someone in North America does a Google search on the word "ghost."
* "Kid-friendly ghosts" is searched nearly 800,000 times a year on YouTube (and there are 4,117,975 #ghost posts on Instagram as I write these words).
* Roughly 40 to 45 percent of the US population believes in ghosts (Harris poll).
* Three in four Americans believe in the paranormal (Gallup).
* Twenty-two percent of Americans say they've felt or seen a ghost (CBS News).

When it comes to the Internet, there are more than 143 million Google entries for "ghost" and more than 32 million results for "ghost photo." The top Google ghost questions include the following:

* What does the Bible say about ghosts?
* How to talk to ghosts.
* What do ghosts look like?
* How old is the belief in ghosts?
* How to overcome fear of ghosts.
* How to summon a ghost.
* What does it mean when you dream about ghosts?
* How to contact ghosts.
* How many people believe in ghosts?
* How to communicate with ghosts.

And then there are the 300 million Buddhists, 800 million Hindus, and millions of assorted "others" who believe in reincarnation. They probably don't even think to ask those questions because the answers are self-evident to them.

We human beings are not just biological matter, we're also comprised of energy. We intimately coexist with the unseen world and its invisible energies, from the force of gravity to invisible waves that transmit every form of media into our lives on a daily basis. Satellites keep our lives buzzing along invisible electronic grids that do everything from making our remote controls work to control tower radar that keeps airplanes from colliding in midair, never mind the miracle of electricity, microwaves, radio, and microchips that are all powered by invisible energy.

So bottom line: If a colonial woman back in the 1600s said to some Puritan dickweed that one day people would have small handheld devices to talk to and see each other in real time from different parts of the planet, you can bet she would have ended up a femme flambé faster than you could say the word "ghost." And if that same woman happened to be a lesbian?

# CHAPTER SIX

# I'm Coming Out—Again

*The single best thing about coming out of the closet is that nobody can insult you by telling you what you've just told them.*

—RACHEL MADDOW

*When someone lives as a minority, they experience the world differently than those of us who live in the majority. We may occupy the same physical space, but we don't occupy the same psychic space.*

—JENNIFER GRANHOLM

Official lesbian leader Ellen DeGeneres made the toaster oven famous to the lesbian world in the "The Puppy Episode" when she came out in her sitcom, *The Ellen Show*. A toaster oven is a marker of a lesbian's sexual experience with a straight woman, as in: If you recruit a straight girl to the wild side, you get a toaster oven. But I got this wrong: I used this term when referring to gay men and actually thought that all lesbians got toaster ovens. (And please don't tell the lesbian police, because they might take my toaster oven back.)

Despite her celebrity status, Ellen's coming out was no picnic.

The network dropped her and she was shunned by many fans until the culture at large finally embraced her for who she truly is. Though I managed to come out without getting ostracized by too many people, coming out as gay is still a wickedly courageous act. Simply speaking, coming out in general is composed of four essential ingredients: 1) You have a secret unlike those of most other people, 2) that secret is counterculture, 3) people are still seriously scorned for it (despite recent strides), and 4) that secret poses perceived religious conflicts for Bible-thumpers and assorted traditionalists.

But if you think that coming out once in life is a lot, imagine coming out twice. Because coming out as a ghost photographer had similar ingredients and was just as scary as coming out as gay. I knew that I'd be scorned or judged or called "woo-woo," "kooky," or "a liar." I actually would have judged a self-proclaimed "ghost photographer" to be odd before my own psychic journey began. My worst fear was that I would lose credibility at work, much like the illustrious Ms. DeGeneres. That didn't happen, fortunately; in fact, quite the opposite took place, though my fear was as real as it was on the day I told an old friend that I was gay in 1993. You gamble, because once you spit out the words, you don't know what response you'll get.

So, gay or ghosts, it doesn't matter—there must be a universal plan out there that assures there's at least one taboo thing about me that makes people uneasy. Take your pick: lesbian or ghost photographer.

In coming out again, I also had to get past my own incredulity about *myself*. I had to believe that what I was experiencing was real. My entire life became a tribute to the wise words of Wayne Dyer: I had to change the way I saw things and what I believed about them.

*There must be a universal plan out there that
assures there's at least one taboo thing about me
that makes people uneasy. Take your pick: lesbian
or ghost photographer.*

⚜

I was already known at work as a renaissance lesbian (that's actually what I call myself, because I'm into arts and crafts and clickers), but adding ghost photographer/mystic-in-training was a different story. After my first reading with Brenda, I flew to Cincinnati to see her for a private four-hour follow-up. Then I returned for another. And another. And another. I hadn't just changed the way I looked at things—the spirit world was tapping me on the shoulder. (Later, it would hit me over the head with a frying pan.) I was not only paying attention, I was on a mission to learn everything I possibly could. I wanted to harness the same superpowers as Brenda and wear a damn cape.

I quickly became Brenda's elf in training. (Brenda calls me an elf because I'm constantly doing and making things. I could live in a tree that I carved out myself *and* bake cookies in it.) On weekends I would fly to Cincinnati to study with Brenda and learn about the tarot, stones, crystals, dowsing rods, and pendulums—five things I'd never strung together into one sentence until just now. At first I felt a little like Keanu Reeves sticking his fingers through the Matrix with his mouth perpetually ajar. Eventually I ended up more like Harry Potter trying to get his shit together at Hogwarts School of Witchcraft and Wizardry—but not before I became the kind of woo-woo cliché that I used to role my eyes at. Particularly after I stumbled on the Crystal Matrix, an amazing metaphysical supply store in LA that was founded by Patricia Bankins, healer, certified past life and regression integration therapist, Reiki master, and high priestess of all things mystical. Patricia quickly became a friend and teacher.

*At first I felt a little like Keanu Reeves sticking his fingers through the Matrix with his mouth perpetually ajar. Eventually I ended up more like Harry Potter trying to get his shit together at Hogwarts School of Witchcraft and Wizardry.*

To be clear, the only crystals I ever had before this time were the wineglasses in my bar. I've always associated them with the New Age movement of the 1970s, which had given them a bad rap along with macramé, patchouli, and too much hair. (Actually, I think macramé should make a comeback. We definitely need a macramé movement.) But if changing the way you look at things changes the things you look at, well, nothing spoke to that reality more than my relationship to crystals.

I knew squat about crystals until I met Patricia, and perhaps you know little about them, too. But like the fossil fuel you put in your car that literally makes your life go round, crystals are some of the earth's most powerful materials. Think about it: Fossil fuel is formed by the decomposition of dead organisms that contain energy from ancient photosynthesis. And those organisms date back hundreds of millions of years. So every time you fill your car with gas or enjoy any of the countless basic amenities we modern humans take for granted, you're essentially tapping into prehistory and an organic world that's as dense and rich as cheesecake.

Crystals, in fact, are even older than the fossils that fuel our world. They are billions of years old, much older than the dinosaurs, going back to the big bang. They grow deep in the earth's crust but are also found in deep space—in fact, as you're reading this, tiny silicate crystals are floating inside icy comets on the edge of our solar system.

And that's just the beginning of the amazing qualities of crystals. These incredible earth gems have bona fide healing and bioelectric properties. Black tourmaline was studied by our illustrious Founding Father Benjamin Franklin for its bioelectric properties, which were later confirmed by the Curies (the folks who studied radiation in the early 1900s). These properties are called "piezoelectricity" and "pyroelectricity," depending on whom you're talking to.

If you have any doubt about how real and powerful they are, consider your basic quartz: Its bioelectric properties are used to regulate the movement and precise frequency of clocks and watches. Quartz is also used to regulate the precise inner workings of microprocessors, radios, solar cells, and other sophisticated technology.

Crystals are comprised of repeating three-dimensional arrangements of atoms, ions, and molecules. They are some of the most elegant and complex expressions of earth chemistry that you can possibly imagine. Your average crystal was growing in a real matrix—a natural material such as soil or rock—as far back as the Precambrian era and will outlive you by billions of years. The oldest known pieces of the earth's surface are 4.4-billion-year-old zircon crystals found in Western Australia. Back then, the earth was *still being formed* by stellar dust and interstellar gases.

When you think about their incredible properties, is it any wonder that crystal balls have been used as divination tools as far back as Celtic Druids? Or that the Christian Church condemned them during medieval times as heretical? Or that people in high political places have used them for divination, including Dr. John Dee, a renowned mathematician, geographer, and consultant to the queen of England in the late 1500s?

⤛⤜

I began to amass the biggest and most badass collection of crystals. My specimens currently include two nuummite skulls, each fifteen and twenty pounds. Nuummite is over three billion years old, found only in Greenland and also considered part of the Earth's first crust, and revered for its transformative qualities. I have different tourmaline stones called liddicoatite found only in Madagascar (that rare crystal comes in stunning colors and really opens up your third eye), as well as extremely potent double-terminated black tourmaline from Sindhupal-chowk (don't worry, I can't pronounce it either), a remote Nepalese mine in the mountainous region outside of Katmandu. I also have selenite wands from the Cave of Swords in Mexico, and enhydros crystals with tiny million-year-old water particles trapped inside. A forty-eight-pound quartz skull from China presides over my office like a special dignitary, flanked by other small crystal skulls in various colors. (I clearly have a thang for crystal skulls.)

I also have two phurbas that were custom made for me by a Tibetan monk. A phurba (pronounced "purr-bah") is a three-sided dagger and Tibetan ritual tool that wards off dark energy. The three sides of the phurba blade are known as the "three poisons": attachment, ignorance, and aversion. In ancient times some of the most prized phurbas were made with what Tibetans called "sky-iron," or tektites and meteorites. Also called a kila, a phurba has energy that's intense and sometimes merciless. Daggers, scepters, sabers—they all look like phurbas and are part of our collective storytelling imagination for a reason. (Spoiler alert: The dagger that brings the Nightwalkers to their knees in *Game of Thrones* is made of dragon glass—aka obsidian.)

My phurbas weren't cheap—they're adorned with coral, turquoise, and a magnificent carved crystal skull—but hey, a girl needs her protection. My home office now feels like a cross between a steampunk saloon and the Emerald City—and, yeah, my road to enlightenment was paved in very expensive stones.

><~><

I spent a year being trained by Patricia in transcrystal therapy, which involves using the bioelectric properties of crystals to heal and integrate the body with the mind-spirit and the emotional self. It also helps sleuth out where emotional trauma may have lodged itself in the physical body. We even had weekly homework that I completed diligently and on time—a far cry from my experience as an ADD student who could only focus on what interested her. (Attention parents: ADD kids are not generalists, so don't expect them to be. They're wildly passionate for and hyperfocus *only* on what interests them at school. So be it. You can't fit a square peg in a round hole.)

I also studied the meaning and dynamics of the chakras (energy centers of spiritual power in our bodies; see appendix five, "The Crystal Kingdom") and, along the way, got in touch with some deep-seated childhood issues I'd been storing in my root (first) chakra like a lot of shitty discount baggage. (I'll open some of that baggage later.) Part of my chakra training included learning the ancient technique of laying of stones and the use of a pendulum, which is a small weight on a chain that can be used to register energy in one's body (energy that might be stuck or need healing) and in larger spaces like houses and rooms. These small wonders have been used throughout the centuries as divination tools for locating water, precious stones, and other key resources. (I now have a small collection of very special pendulums to which I'm fiercely attached.)

⟩〜⟨

At the Crystal Matrix, I also met Ima, a gifted psychic who's studied with some of the most enlightened souls, including many who were taught at the Berkeley Psychic Institute. Ima can see and move energy (without leaving her sofa to do so). She can also talk to the dead, to spirit guides, and to the higher selves of mere mortals like you and me.

Ima taught me a set of psychic tools and practices, one of which is how to properly ground myself. I'm not talking about getting calm and centered through meditation; I'm talking about getting psychically grounded through a visualization technique. I imagine a "grounding cord" that starts at the back of my first chakra (aka the crack of your ass, if you need a visual) and goes down into the center of the earth.

This grounding technique is like having an emotional anchor that aligns body and spirit while connecting you squarely to a deep, steady energy at the earth's core. This not only protects and helps you stay responsive versus reactive in life, you also become more thoughtful, measured, and intentional, while having a keener sense of trust in your intuition, or higher self.

Ima quickly became part of my spiritual posse along with Patricia and Brenda, and the Crystal Matrix my official Weekend Witch Camp. I went from giving away writing utensils at the office to giving away pieces of quartz and black tourmaline. I wore crystals in my bra (blue lace agate, if you must know) to open up my fifth chakra, which is all about communication—so difficult for women in the male-dominated corporate world. Every week the crystals in my office got bigger and more badass. Coworkers would come to complain about physical or emotional struggles, and I'd dole out crystals like candy. Even one of our data scientists who has a PhD in mathematics got psyched when I gave him a big, honking crystal for his desk.

I also used pendulums at work and at cocktail parties and did tarot on bar counters and airplane tray tables. I talked to everyone and anyone about what I was learning. I was a total fucking zealot, an evangelical spirit junkie. I was a little like someone who was color-blind their whole life, then got special glasses that allowed them to see color for the first time. There are vide online that show stupefied people moved to tears when they the world in full color for the first time. The world in black white was their absolute truth; now they suddenly saw the world in colors they couldn't even articulate. They had to understand things like ultraviolet light, infrared, and X-rays, and even learn things about their own vision. Everything they knew to be true was abruptly, radically changed.

Well, folks, that was me. And pretty soon weird shit started to happen that would blow my metaphysical house down once and for all.

# CHAPTER SEVEN

# Mother Always Knows Best

*A mother's love for her child is like nothing else in the world. It knows no law, no pity, it dares all things and crushes down remorselessly all that stands in its path.*

—AGATHA CHRISTIE

One day I'm at the gym on the elliptical machine reading e-mail. (Clearly, I'm not totally engaged in my workout.) As I scan the "sender" list, I see a message from "Chief Warrant Officer Lisa Bryan." Funny enough, Lisa Bryan, or Lisa Vela as I knew her from our Oklahoma days, was one of my babysitters. She's my brother's age, three years older than me. I had just recently found out that she had had a crush on my brother in high school. How cute is that? She could have become Lisa Rieger. I don't think my brother ever knew she had a crush on him, though.

Lisa became very close to my mom while we were growing up in Oklahoma. They would shop together and talk for hours about life. I remember when Lisa came over to talk to Mom about joining the army. It was a very intense conversation. I'm pretty sure they exchanged *I love you*s when they hugged good-bye. Lisa was like family and one of the kindest people you could ever meet, so you can understand my desperation when I read that she'd been diagnosed with uterine cancer. Fucking uterine cancer. *Not her*, I say to myself. *Please not her*.

As my heart breaks my disingenuous workout ends. I just stop moving. I make my way over to the bench press to sit and think about what to do or say to Lisa to help her in this moment of crisis. I have a spiritual "duh" moment: *Of course*, I think, *I'll ask my mom*.

When I started studying with Brenda, she explained how I could communicate with my mother. "Close your eyes and ask your mom to come to you," she said. "She'll show up how she wants you to see her." That's what spooks do, she explained. They show us how they want to be seen, which is not the way we necessarily remember them. This is to make it clear that our minds aren't playing tricks on us. "Start with basic yes and no questions," Brenda added, "and allow her to respond to you." This simplicity is apparently important when you're summoning Spirit. You don't want to start with too many options; it can get confusing. It's like giving a Cheesecake Factory menu to a kid. Don't do it— trust me on this. Just ask: hamburger or hot dog? (Or if you're in LA: vegan dog or tofu chicken?)

For some reason, I haven't actually summoned my mom before, but now in the middle of the noisy, sweaty gym with people in loud Lycra shorts I decide it's time. I feel a little bit like what an electrician must feel like after he's rewired a house and is about to flip the circuit breaker for the first time.

I put my head in my hands, close my eyes, and start to use the grounding technique that Ima taught me. I slowly lose aware-ness of my surroundings: There's no more loud music playing or shiny annoying gym equipment pumping. I enter a solid, serene space with measured intention. Then I simply say inwardly: "Hi, Mom."

I wait.

Within seconds, Mom appears in my mind's eye, almost as if she is superimposed on the ordinary visual world I inhabit. She's beautiful and has long hair. This is weird to me because I never knew her with long hair, but what the hell, her looks are up to her. This reminds me of what Brenda told me about ghosts showing up the way they want to be seen. All that said, my mom *is* wearing the pricey Charlotte Ford jeans she used to wear all the time.

I'm beside myself with joy at the extraordinary sight of my "ordinary" mother, and overcome with a mix of awe and relief. She is no longer on this earthly plane, but I can feel and "see" her now almost as clear as day.

> *I'm beside myself with joy at the extraordinary sight of my "ordinary" mother, and overcome with a mix of awe and relief. She is no longer on this earthly plane, but I can feel and "see" her now almost as clear as day.*

"Mom," I continue, "you may have heard that Lisa is in trou-ble. Is she gonna survive this?"

I see my mom nod yes.

"Okay then. Sweet. Should I go see her?"

Mom shakes her head no.

"Really? Wouldn't she want to see me after surgery?"

Mom shakes her head no.

"Oh, come on. Well. Okay. Will she have a tough surgery?"

Mom answers no.

"An easy one?"

Again, no.

At this point I start to wonder what I'm doing wrong. Based on what I ask so far, Lisa doesn't want me around, and her surgery is going to be neither good nor bad. Maybe I'm no good at this. After all, this is my first time communicating with Mom. Am I fooling myself? I try to keep doubt at bay, but it's not easy.

"Mom," I ask now, a tad awkwardly, "is there something else going on?"

Mom nods yes.

"Okay, now we're getting somewhere. What do I need to ask you, Mom? What am I missing? Oh, I know: Are they going to postpone her surgery?"

Mom shakes her head no.

Oh, for Pete's sake. Clearly I'm not there yet, but I do feel like I'm getting warmer.

"Okay, Mom. Is there something going on with her diagnosis? Does she have something else?"

Mom doesn't respond at all.

"Is there something wrong with her diagnosis?" (I figure two questions at once is a stretch for us at this point.)

Mom nods yes.

"Oh, Mom. The doctors are wrong, aren't they?"

She replies yes.

"Thank you, Mom. I love you."

She nods yes.

Now what do I do? Do I call Lisa? *Hey, Lisa, it's Julie. Got your e-mail. So I decided to consult my dead mother on your diagnosis. She said you're fine for now. Tell the doctor to call Margaret if he doesn't believe you.* Oh hell no, I'm not going to call her with that information. I'll go the chickenshit route and text instead.

"Hi, Lisa. I got your e-mail," I text. "I'm so sorry you're dealing with this. I know this may sound crazy, but I tapped into Mom and asked her about you. She said you will be okay. You may want to check with your doctor about the diagnosis. I love you. Your old babysittee."

What a strange thing I just did. My only solace is that Lisa is of Native American heritage, and I'm banking that her beliefs expand beyond the physical world. Or not. It is a gamble, let's be honest.

A few days later my cell phone rings. The incoming call reads: "Chief Warrant Officer Lisa Bryan." What in the world is she going to say? Naturally, because I am human after all, everything that runs through my head is all bad, all negative. I probably shouldn't have said anything. Ugh.

"Julie, it's Lisa," she says in her soft, sweet voice.

"Hi, Lisa. What's goin' on?" I say like an idiot. I know exactly what's going on.

"Well. I got your text."

Oh boy, here we go. "Yeah, well—" I fumble.

Lisa interrupts. "Julie, you know how much I love your mother. And I want to call and tell you that she was right."

"Wait. What? She was?" I say gleefully, both because Lisa

doesn't have to go through that horror and, of course, because my mom rocks.

"Yeah, it was weird," she continues. "I was in the operating room, getting prepped. All the nurses were there organizing the surgical tools and everything. Then the phone rang. I heard the nurse say, 'Uh-huh, okay, I understand.' After she hung up, she began to put things away while instructing the other nurses to do the same. I asked what was going on. She told me the doctor will be down soon, there was an error with my diagnosis." The relief in Lisa's voice is thick with emotion.

I'm just a wee bit flabbergasted. "You know how much Mom loved you, Lisa. She's still looking after you." I pause for a minute, then admit: "I was scared to death you'd think I was a nut by sending that text."

"Julie, I love that you sent the text. You're a nut with or without texting me."

We both laugh and say "I love you" almost at the same time. I'm reminded how much my mom loved both Lisa and me. Her presence is a reminder that the dead want us to celebrate life. Being human is a sacred experience, even with all the pain. In fact, pain itself is a privilege, too. Because yeah, we all know about love: Love makes the world go round. It really, truly does. And that's why the absence of it is usually the primary source of pain in the human experience.

I'm reminded of this when Lisa and I say our final good-byes and hang up. I'm overjoyed for Lisa's well-being and the incredible access to my mom that came so simply, and yet with such grace and power.

# CHAPTER EIGHT

# A Witch and an Elf Step into a Bar

*Witnessing is the alchemy of enlightenment. It can transform mud into gold.*

—AMIT RAY

Picture this: It's Halloween night in New York City, and I extend a business trip there to spend more time with Brenda, my psychic teacher from Cincinnati (whom I now call the "Good Witch"). Brenda is in Manhattan to do live, in-person group-spirit readings for a gathering of around eighty people à la the *Long Island Medium*. These people are New Yorkers, so they take no bullshit. At least half of them will get a direct message from the Other Side. If they're paying attention, the other half will realize that these messages also have meaning for them.

"You may not get a message tonight," Brenda tells the crowd, "but every message is for you." In other words, pay attention and you'll find personal meaning in whatever Spirit brings forth.

The event takes place in a spacious yoga studio that's clearly made for large practices. (Not that I'd know; I don't practice yoga. My idea of a sun salutation is lying in a lounge chair in cutoff shorts, preferably with a tequila shot.) The event is riveting: People are moved to tears, and astonishment has a vise grip on the crowd as spirits communicate specific information through Brenda in much the same way she conveyed information to me from my parents. The experience never ceases to amaze and move me.

At one point after a break midway through the event, Brenda approaches me and looks right at me as if no one else is in the crowd. "The M Squad came to see me during the break," she says. "They say that if you run into difficult times, remember who you are; keep doing what you're doing."

⨉⌁⌁⨉

The M Squad consists of Mona; my mom, Margaret; and my aunt Marlene. Marlene was my beloved godmother, by the way. She had a tiny body, giant boobs (I always wondered how she didn't tip over while standing up), and fiery red hair. About a year after my mom died, Aunt Marlene got sick. Shortly thereafter, when I was in the tub one night, she appeared in front of me in a sort of vision. She showed me her two kids, then started to fly around and through them. Brenda said this was a sign that Aunt Marlene was ready to pass to the Other Side; sure enough, the next morning she left our good Earth. Ever since then, however, she occasionally pops by for a visit, hence her participation what Brenda refers to as my M Squad.

All the emotion of that evening in New York—the spirits bringing their messages, the humans overcome with feeling—goes right to my stomach. "I'm starving," I say to Brenda after the event. "Let's go grab a bite."

We walk around Lower Manhattan looking for a good chow house and laughing at New Yorkers in their Halloween costumes along the way. We finally stumble into a small quaint café and we're in luck: There's an empty table for two just calling our name. By now it's almost 11:00 p.m. in the city that never sleeps. Brenda and I claim our seats, hers facing out to the center of the café, mine facing the street. As we recount the event that night, I turn to rest my coat on the back of my chair. When I turn back around, I hear a loud *thump*.

I look across the table and Brenda is gone. Where the hell did she go?

I scan the restaurant and finally see her on her knees across the room with her hands lying on a man's body. The guy has fallen backward off his bar stool and is passed out on the floor.

I have no idea what to do until I see the unconscious guy's friend struggling with Brenda. She tries to push him away from her while he tries to push her away from his unconscious buddy. So I get up, pull the friend off of Brenda, and proceed to act like a circus bear. I figure Brenda is doing some woo-woo stuff and needs her space, so I tell the friend: "Dude. Don't worry, she's a professional and knows what she's doing." I say this with total conviction even though I have no idea what's going on.

"Yeah, she's a doctor," I add. I'm going to hell for lying. "He'll be fine." Another ticket to hell. "Oh yeah, she's done this before." Front-of-the-line pass to hell.

The whole time I'm standing like a bouncer between the guy and Brenda. He keeps pressuring me just to let him get his friend and go. Clearly he's paranoid about something sketchy.

The bartender calls the paramedics while a waitress comes

over, squats, and talks to Brenda; then she pulls off her wristwatch and checks the guy's pulse.

The man is just beginning to open his eyes when the paramedics rush in with a stretcher and lots of equipment—and Brenda's job is now done. Once the man is safely in the hands of the paramedics, we sit our asses back down at the table. Nothing like a little midnight Manhattan magic.

"Soooooo . . ." I say. "What the fuck happened?"

"I saw the guy fall backward and hit the floor," Brenda explains. "Then I saw his spirit begin to leave his body."

"Wait . . . you *what*?"

"Well, yeah; I can see spirits, remember?"

"Right, right." Of course, what was I *not* thinking? "Thank you for the reminder," I say.

"So I had to go over to him," she continues. "Normally I ask the spirit if it wants to stay or go. I must honor its wishes."

Sure, why not?

"His spirit was as messed up and confused as his body, so he couldn't really make the call to stay or go. But his spirit was still attached to him, and when that's the case, spirits generally opt to stay in their human bodies. So when I offered the energetic support, that's what happened."

"And then what?"

"And then I waited for you, my elf. Where the hell were you? I needed help."

"Okay, fine. Fair enough, I was a little slow on the uptake. It was my first time being an assistant to a medium. Come on, cut this elf some damn slack."

"Then the waitress came over and asked if I was a doctor," Brenda continues. "I told her that I was more of a healer; she understood and asked what she could do to help, so I asked her to keep an eye on his pulse. And thank you, by the way, my elf. I was ready to throw down his friend."

"You're welcome, my witchy-poo."

"I was relieved when the paramedics arrived; he was already coming back."

Once Brenda finishes her story, I want to ask more questions, but I'm interrupted by a few drunk girls sitting next to us, thanking Brenda for bringing in the hot guys in uniform. (Paramedics and firemen do it every time.) "So how the hell did you move so fast and know what to do?"

"I'm here to serve. I'm here to help. In my mind, there is never a choice."

Oh jeez, how could you not love this woman? Next question: "Brenda, did you ever wonder what the people in the restaurant were thinking?"

"No, I never thought about it. Why?"

"Well, we've all seen *ER* and *Grey's Anatomy*. We mere mortals think that when someone runs to rescue another, they should be giving them CPR or pounding their chest or doing something that TV doctors do. But not you. You're the lady who ran to his side and placed your hands on him and didn't move—not once. How fucked up is that if you're a normal person, sippin' on a mojito, and *bam*—crisis averted by the lady who didn't move?"

"Shit," she says, shaking her head and laughing.

I love this woman. She makes the world better. She makes *me* better. It was an honor that night to be her elf. I witnessed spiritual healing in action. While trick-or-treaters were waltzing all over Manhattan that night, real spirits were moving in and out of human bodies. The drama of life and death, that delicate dance, was playing out like it does a million times a day all over the world. In becoming part of this alchemy in action, I, too, was joining the dance in a curious way.

*I witnessed spiritual healing in action. While trick-or-treaters were waltzing all over Manhattan that night, real spirits were moving in and out of human bodies. The drama of life and death, that delicate dance, was playing out like it does a million times a day all over the world.*

# CHAPTER NINE

# Poltergeist*ish*

*They're here . . .*

—CAROL ANNE,

*POLTERGEIST*

I can't get that New York experience out of my mind; how Brenda held a space for that guy's fugitive spirit, how she saved his life. And then not long after I'm back in Los Angeles, a strange thing happens: It's a Sunday evening, around 10 p.m. I'm snuggled up in bed trying to shed the anticipated Monday morning angst.

"Baby?" Suzanne asks curtly from the bathroom. "Did you touch this when you left here?"

"I haven't been in there, honey, what are you talking about?" I roll out of bed and shuffle to the bathroom. Suzanne is silent, pointing to a hook between two mirrors where I hang my necklaces and pendulum. I immediately know what's wrong: My pendulum is swinging forcefully back and forth like it has its own little internal engine.

"Go," I say to my lovely wife. "I'll take care of this." I'm a big talker, but have no idea what I'm going to do—at least not right now. I do know, however—I just *know*—that we have an uninvited guest from the spirit world in our bathroom. I also know that this guest is not here to be of service to us. I *feel* it. In fact, I'm pretty sure that it was waiting until Suzanne was alone before it made its shitty little self known through the pendulum, because Suzanne is sensitive to these things. She is pure light, and darkness, as I now know, is often attracted to the light.

I instinctively grab my pendulum off the hook, hold it over my palm, and ask it to give me a yes. Normally it should turn clockwise in a circular motion. It does not. It hovers over my palm and shakes like a meth addict looking for a hit.

I grab a bag of sacred Native American sage, light just one leaf, and swing the pendulum through the smoke, talking the entire time in very clear terms. Here's what I say:

*Whatever you are, wherever you came from, if you are not here for the highest good of my family or me, get the fuck out of here. You cannot stay. And when you leave, you are not to touch a hair of one of my dogs or cats. You are to leave my property. You are to leave my people, my place, my things. I wish no harm to you. Find the light and get the fuck out of here.*

And just like that, my pendulum stops and our uninvited invisible guest is gone.

I ask my pendulum again to give me a yes. It circles clockwise. I then ask for a no, and it circles counterclockwise. Finally I ask: "Was that entity malevolent?" It circles clockwise. I stand there in my bathroom and, for the first time, feel a sense of power that I'd never experienced before.

"You're being tested, my elf," Brenda replies when I tell her what happened the next day. Tested for what, exactly?

Shortly after that experience, Suzanne and I go to a psychic fair at the Crystal Matrix because, let's face it, who doesn't love a psychic fair? I sign us up for different tarot and psychic readings.

Mine is with a beautiful and effervescent psychic named Roxane Romero, who's got long blond hair (yeah, like Goldilocks) and wears sparkly jewelry that matches her sparkly eyes. One look at Roxane just makes you feel happy.

Roxane is already talking as she closes the door behind me, but not to me. Presumably she's talking to spirits—who knows? I've learned never to judge a psychic's methods. Then she sits down, still yammering, and grabs one of her many stacks of tarot cards.

"I don't know why," she says before even cutting the cards, "but I'm supposed to tell you something today that you don't know about yourself. Something that will change you." She pauses for a moment, then proceeds to say: "Unlike your wife, who is light and airy, you are more dark and earthy."

*Dark and earthy?*

"What I mean by that is that you draw upon the energy of the earth."

Got it.

"You have the power to control a thousand horses," she adds.

"With all due respect, Roxane," I reply, "I can't get my yellow Lab to come to me when I call his name. How on Earth could I control a thousand horses?"

"You haven't found your calling," she clarifies. "You're not serving humanity the way you should—and you have not healed yourself yet. You must heal yourself first. If you don't, you'll find yourself becoming physically ill on a regular basis."

This strikes an immediate chord. I've dealt with a slew of strange illnesses my whole life. Just prior to my reading with Roxane, in fact, I'd had tubes in my ears for nine months from a severe ear infection that normally only *kids* get. The only tubes I want in my life should be filled with toothpaste. And though in my youth my mind and body lived in two different neighborhoods, you'd have to be living on a rogue planet not to understand the power of the mind on the body's well-being.

"Our minds influence the key activity of the brain," writes author/philosopher Deepak Chopra, "which then influences everything: perception, cognition, thoughts and feelings, personal relationships; they're all a projection of you." If that sounds too mystical, he goes on in to clarify in *The Book of Secrets: Unlocking the Hidden Dimensions of Your Life* that "every significant vital sign—body temperature, heart rate, oxygen consumption, hormone level, brain activity, and so on—alters the moment you decide to do anything . . . decisions are signals telling your body, mind, and environment to move in a certain direction."

Author/healer/woman extraordinaire Louise Hay simplified that whole idea in much of her work, boiling it down to this mantra you might want to adopt as your own: "I do not fix my problems. I fix my thinking. Then problems fix themselves."

It's hard to break patterns and change your mind-set in one moment, but that's pretty much what happened to me. In the midst of my overwhelming grief, Brenda had blown my mind open. When people grieve, writes medium Concetta Bertoldi in *Inside the Other Side*, they become seekers "even if they weren't seekers before. Even though it's painful, grief can create such an opening in the heart that it allows for truly revolutionary evolution and growth."

*It's hard to break patterns and change your mind-set in one moment, but that's pretty much what happened to me.*

When Roxane told me that I have powers, I knew that she wasn't talking about magic card tricks. I realize now that I experienced a taste of those powers in my bathroom that night. I had already become a seeker, and because I'd committed to the quest more powers were coming my way. And so when Roxane made it clear that my life would be rather unfun if I don't heal myself and use my powers to heal others, I believed her. I don't want my life to end up unfun. I love fun.

Just before our session is over and I'm getting up to leave, Roxane stops me. "Your soul is screaming at you," she insists. "Listen to it."

CHAPTER TEN

# Holy Shit, I Activated a Portal. *Wait*: What's a Portal?

> *Have you ever looked at something and it's crazy, and then you looked at it in another way and it's not crazy at all?. . . Don't be scared. Just don't be scared.*
>
> —ROY NEARY, *CLOSE ENCOUNTERS OF THE THIRD KIND*

Quantum physics has a lot to do with quantifying invisible energy. No one has figured out exactly what black holes are, for example, but few scientists doubt their existence, even though we can't see them with the naked eye. In describing dark energy, an article on the science blog *Live Science* tells us that "astrophysicists have proposed an invisible agent that counteracts gravity by pushing space-time apart" and describes the possibility of "infinitely large 'quilted universes'" and "cosmic patches exactly the same as ours (containing someone exactly like you)."

If your identical twin floating in an intergalactic "cosmic patch" isn't incredible enough, consider this: Quantum physics has gone so far into the cosmic wilderness that some quantum physicists like Hans-Peter Dürr and Amit Goswani speculate that behind the material world there is a hyperspace that can be regarded as an afterlife or a heaven.

This bears repeating, my friends: *Behind the material world there is a hyperspace that can be regarded as an afterlife or a heaven.* And I think that hyperspace might be my backyard.

~~~

So picture this: It's the spring of 2014. I come home from work one day to find that Suzanne has installed a few new bird feeders in our backyard. Our house is located on a corner lot in the hills of Sherman Oaks with a view of the San Fernando Valley from the backyard. The outer perimeter of our lot is covered in ivy (what lurks in that ivy is spookier to me than any ghosts); its focal point is a freeform-shaped swimming pool surrounded by cement and a wooden fence. Not a blade of grass to be found.

We now have around eight bird feeders in our yard that usually attract finches, hummingbirds, blue jays, doves, chickadees, grosbeaks, sparrows, and an occasional hawk. But for some strange reason back then we'd gone through weeks of total feeder vacancy. That's when Suzanne said to me, "Honey, conjure me up some birds."

Suzanne is convinced that I have powers, and now she wants birds.

I'm told by my spiritual posse to trust my instincts, and my instincts tell me to soak clear crystal points in animal spirit oil blend (yup), then lay them in a pattern by each bird feeder. I can't explain why. Really, I can't. It's why they are called "instincts" and not "instructions." I also can't explain what's in that animal spirit oil, either, though I will tell you that I found it on Etsy (yup again).

I love Etsy, by the way. It's a digital version of a western trading post. Back in the day those trading posts used to be roughly twenty miles away from one another—twenty miles being as far as a man could run or ride his horse in one day, get what he needed, and make it back home. Thankfully, these days I don't need a horse. I can just sit my ass down in front of my computer and look for stuff. And who knew that you could find magic potions there? (You can also find cane toad leather coin purses and hand-knit socks for your chair legs. Go figure.)

Within days we go from having only a few bird visitors to having so many flocks of them that their chirping can be heard from the bottom of our neighborhood hill.

Success! Suzanne wanted birds, Suzanne got her birds.

The next few weeks are a whirlwind. After a business trip to New York I meet Suzanne in Cincinnati, then we head to New Orleans for a quick visit to celebrate Easter. We love New Orleans; it has such a beautiful and complicated soul. Normally we let our hair down there, which is code for drinking heavily, staying out incredibly late, and stumbling back to the hotel. This trip is far tamer. No strip clubs. No drag shows. No last calls. I'm far more interested in dropping pennies wherever we go and hitting up Suzanne for extras. (I've been doing this ever since I heard the story of a friend's father who dropped pennies from Heaven everywhere he went.) That weekend in New Orleans I must have dropped at least fifty of them, and at least another five bucks in silver coins. I get a little carried away, but

I love the idea of offering good luck to complete strangers and suggesting that a loved one or an angel is looking over them. It just feels right.

Our flight arrives back in LA on Easter night. It's nice to be home again; I'd missed our little beasts: three dogs and two cats. Every time we pull into the driveway, the barking brigade greets us. Never fails. Homer, the yellow Lab, is my baby. Suzanne got him for me after our studio released *Marley & Me*. I'd never had a dog before. (The German shepherd that sunk its teeth into the back of my five-year-old head was the reason for the delay.) Peggy is the replacement for Suzanne's dog, Punky, who was killed by a coyote one Christmas Day. And Rebel, our mini Maltese, is small and in charge.

Then there are the felines: Booger is one of the greatest cats ever to walk the earth. He loves all. Weirdly, people who are allergic to cats are not allergic to Booger and they all want to take him home. Then there's Tiny Pants, our asocial cat who's so fat that his two-toned paws make him look like he's wearing (you guessed it) really tiny pants.

After our animal greeting we settle in: check the mail, take the bags back to the bedroom, grab a bottle of water. And that's when I see this crazy fucking thing in our kitchen: a giant bird imprint on the window. Like nothing we've ever seen, it looks like a bird slammed into our window going fifty miles per hour. We can see every detail: head, body, wingspan, and feathers; even its beak.

How could a bird have crashed into our kitchen window and left that kind of imprint, we wonder. And where did its body go? Did it have anything to do with the conjuring of birds I'd done weeks earlier?

I take a picture of it with my iPhone and then, as usual, I reach out to Brenda. I text her the photo of what I now call the "bird stain" and the text messaging begins the next morning:

> *Me:* A bird didn't see the window. No remains, though. Crazy, huh? Good weekend? Xoxo.
> *Brenda:* Enlarge the photo. See the face in the glass in the center upper left?
> *Me:* The face of the bird?
> *Me (again):* Ah . . . to the left the bird face?
> *Me (again, clearly text bombing her):* I see something in the purple. Like a woman.

In fact, I see the spooky spectral figure of a cloaked woman with a pointy chin and a slightly tormented expression.

> *Me:* OMG. It looks kinda spooky. Who is that? Or *what* is that? What the hell, witchy-poo?
> *Brenda:* It's your spook message! Definitely cool.
> *Me:* Ah come on.

I look back at the window, then back down at the image on my phone. That spectral image is as clear as day, even though the pic was shot at night: A spirit is clearly hovering there—wherever "there" really is—as if it were waiting to be seen. How long has this invisible houseguest been hanging around? Is it really possible that I conjured up some ghosts along with Suzanne's birds?

"Birds are messengers," Brenda tells me much later. Clearly, this bird had a message.

❦

Ghost or spirit photography has been around since the invention of the camera. The most famous ghost pic—or one of the earliest, at least—was of a bunch of adorable winged fairies dancing around two young cousins in the English countryside in 1917 called the *Cottingley Fairies*. They caught the attention of Sir Arthur Conan Doyle, best known as the creator of our beloved Sherlock Holmes. Doyle was a serious spiritualist who was fascinated with the paranormal and regularly consulted mediums and psychics. He was also a founding member of the Hampshire Society for Psychical Research in 1889 and involved with similar organizations, including the Ghost Club in London.

Those *Cottingley Fairies* ghost photographs were quickly proved to be fakes, which isn't a surprise. We humans love to fake things, from boobs to news. Ever since those fairies, however, people have been taking countless ghost photographs, some of which you'll see again and again on the Internet. There's the seriously freaky *Amityville Horror Ghost* pic that inspired the movie, and the *Brown Lady*, who's said to be the spirit of Lady Dorothy on a staircase. (Lady Dorothy was locked in a closet by her husband and left to die after she discovered his infidelity. I'd haunt that fucker, too, if I were in her spirit shoes.) The list goes on: There's Lord Combermere's ghost from 1891, the FAF officer Freddy Jackson from 1919, the *Backseat Driver* from 1959, the *Tulip Staircase* ghost, the so-called *Corroboree Rock Spirit*, and the *Colonial Park Cemetery* ghost.

If you dig online you'll find these pics and all kinds of fleeting images caught on trail cameras in night forests, unexplained faces of strangers in rooms where no one was present, outlines of people standing, hovering, staring, or otherwise making their baffling astral presence known only after a photo was developed. Some of these photos are fakes that have been explained away as double exposures, lens flares, or, more recently, Photoshop, but others persist as unexplained mysteries.

⤝⤞

All that said, when I take my first ghost photograph I am seriously spooked. I am not a "ghost hunter," nor do I aspire to be one. The only reason I'm not running around the neighborhood with my hair on fire screaming, *Lock your door, hide your kids, we've got ghosts!* at that moment is because of Brenda. That magical woman, my psychic Sherpa, can navigate the unseen world better than any human can navigate the physical world.

Still, at first I don't tell anyone what's going on because I figure they'll think I'm batshit crazy. But every night I go into my backyard and try to capture pics of spooky wildlife like some sort of gonzo *National Geographic* photojournalist trying to spot a snow leopard. Whatever I see, I take a photo of it: my dog, the swimming pool, potted plants, empty rooms, every corner of every space—even selfies. I'm literally moonlighting in moonlight every night, periodically checking my sanity with Brenda.

Brenda assures me that it's not that unusual to capture spirit entities on film or clearly see them where others see nothing. "It's not a big deal if you have eyes to see," she says, "but not everyone *does* have eyes to see." When I ask her why that spirit might have shown up in the photo with the bird stain, she suggests that I might have somehow activated a portal. (She also wondered why the fuck I was soaking crystals in animal spirit oil that I bought on Etsy.)

*Brenda assures me that it's not that unusual to
capture spirit entities on film or clearly see them
where others see nothing. "It's not a big deal if you
have eyes to see," she says, "but not everyone does
have eyes to see."*

Naturally I inquire: "What is this said portal you speak of? The only portal I know of is Yahoo. Surely you're not talking about the Internet."

"You know, my little elf," she replies, "a portal is an opening to the Other Side, like when you use a Ouija board—don't ever do that; they're bad—or like the ones in the movie *Poltergeist*." (Apparently, Ouija boards can invite dark energy into a room.)

Uh, did she just say "poltergeist"? I'm just a tad flabbergasted, because little did Brenda know (or maybe she "knew" in her psychic way) that at that very moment my studio team was in the early stages of developing the marketing pitch for the remake of the original *Poltergeist*.

Here's a brief summary for those of you who haven't seen *Poltergeist*: A nice, "normal" American family is living in a generic Southern California suburban house that they eventually find out was built on a cemetery. Their young daughter, Carol Anne, discovers a portal in her closet and gets abducted by a poltergeist. Things rapidly go to hell—kinda literally. Turns out they not only have a poltergeist in their house, they have a whole Rotary Club of ghosts lingering around from a "sphere of consciousness" that's identified by a medium. (Talk about bringing your property value down.) Things go from bad to worse when their son, Robbie, is attacked by a clown doll in his bedroom in what's gone down as number 80 in Bravo's *100 Scariest Movie Moments*. (Like I've always said: Never trust a clown.)

Okay, so never mind that I actually happen to live in a Southern California suburban house, or that life imitates art—an expression that will soon become a massive understatement in my world. At the time all I want to understand was this: What exactly *is* a portal?

According to *Supernatural Magazine*, a portal is "a doorway in the physical world that allows free access to and from the spirit world. The existence of a portal can rely on a vortex of energy to sustain it." Magnetic, spiritual, and other unknown sources like gravitational anomalies can create "powerful eddies that manifest a spiral of energy which can be positive or negative in nature."

Some paranormal specialists believe that portals occur near large bodies of water (hello, swimming pool), because water has a tendency to absorb energy from an emotionally charged event. Everyone knows that water can conduct electricity, so it stands to reason that it might also "charge" spirits and ghosts to manifest in the physical world. It can also charge the life out of us humans, which is why you'll immediately fry like a drumstick if you're hit by lightning when you're in a pool or the ocean. And never mind what happens if you drop your hair dryer in the sink when it's plugged into your wall socket.

Now, there's a difference between a poltergeist and a ghost. According to the Merriam-Webster dictionary, a ghost is "a disembodied soul; especially the soul of a dead person believed to be an inhabitant of the unseen world or to appear to the living in bodily likeness." Simple enough. When these "disembodied souls" stick around to protect and guide us, not haunt us, they become our guardian angels.

Poltergeists, on the other hand, are pissy bitches. They're angry about some transgression and they're coming back to give you shit by creating physical disturbances: breaking objects, knocking on doors or walls, even making things levitate. People have been baffled by their presence for centuries; scientists have tried to explain them away as a manifestation of everything from seismic activity, ball lightning, and underground water movement to electromagnetic fields, unusual air currents, and regular old hallucinations. Parapsychologists, those folks who dedicate their life to this, consider them disembodied low-level spirits associated with the natural elements of fire, air, water, and earth.

Any way you look at portals, psychics and mediums are careful when they're messing around with them. They always recite protection prayers to make sure that they're carefully opened *and* securely closed, because apparently they can be left open for hundreds of years, especially if dipshits—I mean inexperienced mere mortals—open them by accident. And that's why I jump into action when Brenda clarifies that opening a spirit portal is like putting out a welcome mat for dark spirits as well as friendly ones. In other words, if you open one, you'd better close it, too.

"Protect yourself and your space," she says. "Always protect your space. Follow my house-clearing instructions word by word." (See instructions in appendix one, "Protect Your Space.") In no time, I become a house-clearing devotee.

# Holy Smoke!

*The so-called dead are still alive. Our friends are still
with us. They guide and strengthen us when owing to
absence of proper conditions they cannot make their
presence known.*

—ALFRED RUSSEL WALLACE

*Now about those ghosts: I'm sure they're here, and
I'm not half so alarmed at meeting up with any of
them as I am at having to meet the live nuts I have to
see every day.*

—BESS TRUMAN

*Behind every man now alive stand thirty ghosts, for that
is the ratio by which the dead outnumber the living.*

—ARTHUR C. CLARKE

Now let's be clear: House clearing and house*cleaning* are not
the same thing. I haven't done a load of laundry since 1993, and
I've never washed a window in my life. (For the record, I *do* wash
dishes.) House clearing involves using various ancient healing
tools to free a house or space of negative energy, whether that
energy comes from emotional trauma experienced in that space

or from errant ghosts and dark energies that have hitchhiked their way into a place for whatever reason.

There are some basic tools involved in house clearing: Black tourmaline has been used since time immemorial to protect people and spaces from dark energy. I buy that by the truckload from my Nepalese source and put it in key areas of a house: near doors, halls, corners, shelves, and bedside tables.

Smudge sticks generate healing smoke and snuff out any bad shit. They're composed of dried herbs—sage, lavender, sweet grass, lemongrass, etc.—tied with string. I carry a candle in case the smudge stick goes out and a feather to ritualistically fan the smoke around a room. I use a turkey feather, but you can use a fan or thick piece of paper. I also use a shell to pick up any ashes from the burning smudge stick because its connection to water rounds out the elements: fire from the burning smudge stick, air from the fanning, and earth from the herbs.

I'm thrilled to buy and burn mountains of sage, by the way, because I like to burn stuff. First off, I was born in the month of August, so I'm a Leo, one of the four fire signs. My love of fire wasn't up to me; I was born this way. This love occasionally got the best of me when I was a kid: for example, I almost burned down a subdivision in my small Oklahoma town when I didn't listen to my mom.

I'm equally thrilled to buy and burn pounds of palo santo sticks as part of my house-clearing arsenal. Palo santo literally means "holy wood." Like sage, it's been used forever by South American healers and shamans for its medicinal and therapeutic healing powers: It spiritually purifies, clears energy, and heals. (Don't ask me why or how. Maybe it has something to do with its rich supply of phytochemicals and antioxidants.) I have bowls filled to the brim with palo santo sticks and give it away in zip-pered bags. (Some people give cookies. I give holy wood.)

The world can't have enough palo santo. The world can't get enough holy smoke, for that matter.

When you read about house clearing, you probably associate it with ghost hunting and think of the same thing I do: ectoplas-mic proton packs and possibly the giant Stay Puft Marshmallow Man from *Ghostbusters*. One of these items sounds rather deli-cious. Who doesn't like a s'more, right? But in all seriousness, ghost hunting is big business, with numerous sites that sell all kinds of gear. My favorite is the BooBuddy Jr., an EMF-triggered (electromagnetic field) stuffed bear that detects changes in en-ergy and even comes with its own carrying case for another eigh-teen bucks. (I'm a sucker for a good custom carrying case. Hats off to the folks who thought of this and bothered to follow through with their dream.)

If I were a real ghost hunter, I'd not only have a BooBuddy, I'd also have an EVP (electronic voice phenomenon) wrist recorder, laser grid scope, spirit box (so ghosts can talk to you), and a ghost rover cam. Oh, and a thermal camera. You can't be a ghost hunter without a thermal camera. However, I do not possess any such clever items for my ghost hunting, and I don't really consider myself a ghost hunter, either. I did once purchase a thermal ghost pad on Amazon. It's almost the size of a sheet of paper and is supposed to turn colors if a ghost touches it. All I got was a paw print of our very living seventy-five-pound yellow Lab.

<center>~~~~</center>

Fully geared up with my house-clearing arsenal, I start a ritual of burning sage and palo santo in my backyard every night. Not once has a single firefighter come pounding at my door to inquire about the giant plume of fragrant smoke perpetually drifting off the hills from our place. (Imagine my surprise, though, if one *did* show up and I simply said: *Hello, dear firefighter. No worries, I'm just smoking out ghosts.* On second thought, this is LA, so said firefighter would probably just roll his eyes and say: *Okay, lady, whatever.*)

One day I find a great new smudge pot, an oil-burning device that's used in certain spiritual rituals to cleanse the energy in a space. (They were originally used to prevent frost on fruit trees.) I walk the perimeter of our property, always with Homer by my side. After a big round of smudging that night, I have so much sage left in my pot that I need to sit down and wait while it burns itself out. While waiting, naturally I get bored, so I start randomly taking pictures of the smoke with my cell phone. And that's when I learn that smoke is to spirits what light is to invisible ink, because I suddenly see in my shots various ghost images that resemble the spirit woman in the "bird stain" shot.

What is it about smoke?

In *Ghosts Among Us*, renowned medium James Van Praagh writes briefly about spirits that make contact with us through photography. "I have seen many photographs showing white orbs or what look like wisps of smoke around figures in a photo," he writes. "Many people think their photos have been ruined. However, I believe that somehow ghosts have impressed a portion of their energy on the electromagnetic energy of the photograph."

Van Praagh could just as well have said that the electromagnetic energy of ghosts somehow impresses itself around smoke. No one knows for sure how or why, but somehow they seem able to pull smoke around their energetic bodies in order to make themselves visible. One thing is for sure: Smoke has always been considered a sacred element. "Since the dawn of time we've been fascinated by smoke," writes spiritual healer and author Jenny Smedley in an article titled "Sacred Smoke & Symbolism of Smoke in Different Traditions" on the website Holisticshop.co.uk. "It seems to symbolize our constant striving to reach the heavens, or the beings that might dwell there. Since man first turned his eyes skyward, smoke has been used as a conduit for prayers, seen as the souls of the dead rising into heaven, for energy shifting and even communication."

*Van Praagh could just as well have said that the electromagnetic energy of ghosts somehow impresses itself around smoke. No one knows for sure how or why, but somehow they seem able to pull smoke around their energetic bodies in order to make themselves visible. One thing is for sure: Smoke has always been considered a sacred element.*

The "beings that might dwell there"?

Smedley cites the Vikings, Aboriginals, Native Americans, Taoists, and of course Christians and the Catholic Church for their use of smoke in sacred rituals. For millennia, when "primitive cultures burned their dead," they saw in the rising smoke "the material manifestation of the soul's journey." Smoke is clearly a medium of detecting energy (and ghosts *do* have energy) much in the way that crystal balls, pendulums, and other divination tools can detect energy. This is a form of scrying, by the way—the practice of seeing messages or images through various mediums, be it a crystal ball, a reflective surface, or smoke.

❧

Pretty soon I'm taking hundreds of ghost photos in smoke with my iPhone, and sure enough, there is something in virtually every picture—and more than just one image. At first I see outlines. I see them shooting out of the pool and on top of the umbrella in our yard. I see one thing that looks like an ape sitting on one of our lounge chairs. Sometimes things appear as colors—purple and green—that aren't visible when I'm taking the picture. I see these colors and outlines everywhere, even through our fence, as if something were peering at me through the slats. I nearly drive patient Suzanne crazy because I won't let her sleep; I lie in bed every night examining photographs, asking what she sees. She never sees what I do; she always sees angels. (I might have left her alone if she'd agreed with my initial assessment of a particular ghost in a photo.)

Anyhow, I don't know who or what these ghosts are, but I clearly must have activated a big-ass portal, because more humanlike images appear: I catch a ghost that looks like he'd had the crap beat out of his face. When I first see him, I feel a sense of deep despair. I find a sweet-looking couple in my sage pot: Each one is resting their head on the other. (He has a long face and she has a rounder face with what looks like curly hair.) I call the photo *Death Is for Quitters*. I also catch a "pirate" with a horizontal knife tip under his nose. God knows what his story is. It's almost like the neighborhood spirits got to a fork in the road, and instead of going right to the local Whole Foods, took a left and ended up at the lesbians' house.

But then, after a while, a strange thing happens: I start to capture not just human-looking entities; I start to capture, well, *creatures*.

Remember how some quantum physicists have speculated that hyperspace could be regarded as an afterlife or a heaven? Well, now I'm *really* wondering if that hyperspace isn't in my backyard, because the most unusual and fantastic-looking entities are starting to show up. In addition to photographing lots of animals (lions, tigers, bears, and a rat), I also capture a row of dancing chickens in one image. Yes, dancing chickens, dancing *ghost* chickens. In fact, the dancing chickens have an audience, or as I like to call them, "the dancing chicken club." One of them looks like Stewie from *Family Guy*, another like a Keystone Kop. I start to capture entities that look like fairies, elves, the Muppets, princesses, princes, centaurs, dragons, and things that are hard to identify but that fascinate me. They look familiar— but not. Some look like they are looking at me, like really *seeing* me.

A few have lights for eyes, like a creature I call "King Frog." (His eyes look like lights and mesmerize me. He also has a club or scepter, because he's a king, after all.) Other entities just pop their heads out of the smoke. One photo shows a man with a full head of hair, a stick body, and two flipper feet. I call him "Wolfman."

I also start to see entities in the swimming pool. The pool activity is insane. I shit you not. These entities or creatures look more magical than scary. I saw a prince and princess atop a mythical centaur-looking figure with a face of an old wise man who looks like a wizard.

It is undeniably strange to see so many of these creatures in my photographs, and rationalizing what might be happening just doesn't pan out. I'm still stuck on how much they look like they stepped out of a fairy tale. They're so fantastic looking that I simply call them "fantasticals," even though some of them look like familiar elves and gnomes, which might not be as wild as you think. Ever since we humans have recorded our history on stone tablets and papyrus, people have seen and documented the presence of mystical "little people," be they Menehunes in Hawaii, aluxes in Central America, trolls and gnomes in northern Europe, or elves in Iceland. Many cultures believe that these tiny earthspirit creatures and protectors of our planet actually exist in our dimension and are simply difficult to perceive with our limited senses. Like poltergeists (only a whole lot friendlier), these supernatural creatures often make themselves known when we are dicking around with our environment and messing with sacred sites.

Elves are such a big part of Icelandic culture, by the way, that the Icelandic Road and Coastal Administration actually builds highways with sacred sites in mind and has a standard five-page reply for the press. It states, among other things, that it "cannot be denied that belief in the supernatural is occasionally the reason for local concerns. . . . We value the heritage of our ancestors, and if oral tradition passed on from one generation to the other tells us that a certain location is cursed, or that supernatural beings inhabit a certain rock, then this must be considered a cultural treasure."

Did you get that, folks? Elves are a cultural treasure in Iceland.

An *Atlantic* article titled "Why So Many Icelanders Still Believe in Invisible Elves" suggests that people in Iceland believe modern humans have become disconnected from "the inner life of the earth," as one Icelander is quoted. "When elves act out," she said, "they are doing more than just protecting their homes, they are reminding people of a lost relationship. They're . . . protectors of nature, like we humans should be. We've just forgotten."

Ain't that the truth?

Obviously we've "just forgotten" a lot of stuff. Clearly Icelanders and other cultures that revere earth spirits have a purer relationship to nature than we do. We're the ones, us New Worlders, who've forgotten about our relationship to Mother Earth, aka Gaia, our true home.

# CHAPTER TWELVE

# House Clearing Like a Hooker

*When I was a little kid, I wrote this play
about all these characters living in a haunted
house. There was a witch who lived there, and
a mummy. When they were all hassling him,
this guy who bought the house—I can't believe
I remember this—said to them, "Who's paying
the mortgage on this haunted house?" I thought
that was really funny.*

—MINDY KALING

I start offering my house-clearing services to anyone remotely interested in them. I'm an equal-opportunity house clearer and carry my protection arsenal wherever I go: smudge sticks, feather fan tool, black tourmaline. With my tendency to blurt, I come right out with it: "Hi! I'm learning how to clear houses. Do you want your house cleared?"

Who's going to say no to that? Nobody.

Soon enough, I'm putting hundreds of miles on my car driving all over Southern California. I clear big and small houses; condos and RVs; hotels and motels; offices and corridors.

Once I'm in a space, I always start at the bottom or lowest level and work my way up. I sit down on the floor, light my candle, and take three deep breaths, allowing my thoughts to clear and my inner/energetic body to expand with each breath. I set my intention, light my smudge stick with my candle, let it burn about thirty seconds, and gently blow out the flame. Then with the smoke trail I "trace" the seams of each room like I'm using a stick of incense. I go from the floor-to-wall seams, up all seams to the ceiling, using my feather tool to send smoke up along them. I also smudge the seams of windows, doorways (of rooms and closets), bookshelves, and mirrors. Waving my smudge stick or using the fan, I make the infinity sign, because it's a perfectly balanced symbol that represents empowerment; I outline the sign with my smudge stick on staircases, over mirrors, and over drains (sinks, toilets, showers, bathtubs, washing machines, dishwasher) the same way. This symbol is particularly helpful in corners under furniture, or any place else energy feels "stuck."

Then I say a protection prayer to safeguard the space (see appendix one, "Protect Your Space"). You can use whatever prayer aligns you with a sense of the divine, but here's my favorite one from Brenda:

> *I bring down a ray of divine light filled with love and protection. I draw a circle around my energetic body. Into the circle I place the white light of peace, the blue light of healing, the clear red light of energy, and the golden light of God. I direct that nothing and no one shall come between my circle and me. And so it is. Amen.*

I learned from Brenda to move counterclockwise inside rooms to move energy out, and clockwise inside to move energy in. Once I feel that the energy has cleared, I'll sometimes say another prayer of gratitude for the spirits that assisted me. Occasionally I leave a small trail of sea salt around a house or property because it acts as a natural purifier; some suggest that it actually absorbs negative energy. I also sometimes leave my smudging tools outside a front door as a reminder to any spirits with the audacity of even *thinking* about creeping back in. And guess what? The air is almost always around 50 percent lighter after a space is cleared.

Brenda has given me a few other indispensable insights. It's a huge privilege to be in a human body, which reminds me of a famous saying by French Jesuit philosopher Pierre Teilhard de Chardin: "We are not human beings having a spiritual experience. We are spiritual beings having a human experience."

I take this understanding about the seniority and authority we have over spirits quite seriously—and get bolder in my assertions as I house clear. Once a room is complete, I sometimes open a window or door and practically yell with conviction: *Anything unaligned to my highest good, leave now!* (Sometimes I'll simply cut to the chase and tell certain asshole spirits to fuck *off*—but I'm getting ahead of myself.)

Soon enough, prayer becomes an integral part of my spiritual practice.

>~~<

God only knows (pun sort of unintended) that a lot has been written about the power of prayer. Danish philosopher Søren Kierkegaard once said: "Prayer does not change God, but it changes he who prays." Spiritual teacher Iyanla Vanzant took it a few steps further: "In my deepest, darkest moments," she wrote, "what really got me through was a prayer. Sometimes my prayer was 'Help me.' Sometimes a prayer was 'Thank you.' What I've discovered is that intimate connection and communication with my creator will always get me through because I know my support, my help, is just a prayer away."

Replace the word "creator" with whatever higher force rocks your world, and you'll start tapping into the true power of prayer.

This, of course, was totally off my radar for most of my life. As a kid I knew the Lord's Prayer by rote, but didn't really pay attention to it. I was mostly interested in getting some of that "daily bread" after church (preferably the unwholesome white kind that you tear off the crust and roll into a walnut-size ball before stuffing into your mouth).

But then one fine day, all that changed. I'm clearing our house and feel the unwelcome presence of *something* or someone. The air suddenly feels dense and fear rolls through every cell in my body. Without premeditation, I begin to recite the Lord's Prayer. I'm deeply committed to the process, but a part of me is still thinking: *WTF? Did years of being an acolyte as a kid and doing sit-stand-kneel calisthenics suddenly pay off?*

I'm not sure what's going on, but as soon as I say, "Our Father who art in Heaven," the fear vanishes. To put it simply, I've suddenly harnessed the power of prayer like I never experienced in church. And as quickly as it reenters my life, it becomes a forceful positive incantation.

Now I realize that for some the Lord's Prayer can be a trigger, depending on your religious affiliation (or lack thereof). But you don't have to use any formal prayer per se to harness that power; anything will do (except, say a dirty limerick), as long as it's said with conviction in evoking a higher force. You can say the Lord's Prayer or you can do the Buddhist om mani padme hum or any protection prayer, words, incantation, or mantra that resonates with you. Hey, you can make your own—as long as you're sincerely connecting to a power greater than you. (Do a Google search on "protection prayers" and thirty million entries come up.)

For me, however, the Lord's Prayer not only becomes one of my tools, it becomes a sort of psychic divining rod. If I recite the prayer while I'm clearing a space and forget the words at any point, that's a sure sign that either a ghost or a not-so-friendly dark energy is present.

This *really* blows me away and comes home to me when I'm space clearing our friend Stephanie's house. As I'm reciting the Lord's Prayer while smudging in her office, I stop in front of a painting and draw a total blank. I suddenly can't remember one single word of the prayer for the life of me. I look over at Stephanie. "What's with this painting?" I ask. "It's stopping me—but not in a bad way. Is there a significance to it?"

"My uncle made that painting," she says, looking a little awestruck. "He was a priest." Turns out she and her uncle were very close. No doubt he recited the Lord's Prayer on a daily basis for most of his life, and as I'm standing there in front of his painting, I get a distinct "sense" from him. When I say "him," I mean that his energy, his spirit, is somehow clear and palpable. That "sense" is that he feels ignored.

"He just wants you to talk about him more, Steph," I reply.

Stephanie shakes her head and confirms she hasn't spent much time connecting with him since he passed.

A few weeks later at Stephanie's birthday party, I recount to her friend Kenna how I drew a blank in front of that painting while saying the Lord's Prayer; her eyes light up like neon saucers. "That's how my mom started off being a psychic!" she says.

Turns out Kenna's mother is a well-known psychic in the Dallas area and was written up in the *Dallas Morning News* some time ago. In the life-imitates-art department, a few weeks later I go to see the movie *The Witch*. I love horror flicks, by the way, but not the bloody disgusting ones, only the psychological or paranormal kind. *The Witch* is a paranormal tale based on a real New England family in the 1630s that was ripped apart by witchcraft and freaky satanic spirits. Produced by Jay Van Hoy, the movie was meticulously researched and reenacted down to the literal seams of the clothes worn by early colonists. Van Hoy even drew from a collection of Elizabethan witch pamphlets he found in the New York Public Library.

In one pivotal scene, the father circles the family around his son, who's possessed by a demon, and demands that everyone recite the Lord's Prayer. Halfway though the prayer, his other two children (young twins) fall to the ground writhing and become catatonic, saying that they forgot the words to the Lord's Prayer. Why? Turns out they're *also* possessed by demons along with their older brother.

Now, I get it—it's a movie. I know the difference between "based on a true story" and "inspired by true events." I also know that the Lord's Prayer isn't kryptonite or a silver bullet that instantly sets off one's psychic awareness of spirits. That said, after these first few experiences I'm starting to *really* pay attention. And nothing grips my attention more than an experience I have in the house of one particular friend.

⤜∼⤛

Meet thirtysomething Alex Van Camp. If you look up the word "handsome" in a dictionary, you'll find Alex. Alex is the epitome of the word. He's more handsome than Ryan Gosling or Ryan Reynolds. In fact, he's more handsome than all Ryans combined. Naturally, his wife is the epitome of the word "pretty." Even her name sounds pretty: Dawn. Honestly, can you imagine an unattractive person named Dawn? She is blond and blue-eyed and has a yoga body. Get the picture?

Alex and I met when he was an ad salesman. I found out early in our relationship that he thought I was a supreme bitch the first time we met. It's true, I can be tough as nails at work. Sometimes, admittedly, I come across as bitchy. Okay, *fine*—I can be a total bitch and I don't suffer fools well. Shoot me.

A year or so after our first alleged bitchy encounter, our mutual friend Meredith asked us both out for drinks. Unbeknownst to me, Alex made an agreement with his wife to call him at a certain time so he had an excuse to bail, not wanting to waste any more time with this bitchy woman. The three of us sit down with our cocktails and begin to talk.

After whipping out my pendulum to read their chakras and make sure they're aligned (more on that in appendix five, "The Crystal Kingdom"), I naturally start to force myself on Alex, suggesting that I come over and clear his house. Meredith encourages him, so he gives in. A few weeks later Suzanne and I head to Alex and Dawn's condo down in Manhattan Beach. I have my bag full of space-clearing tricks: sage, feather, abalone shell, and lighter. For some reason, I also grab some holy water, blessed salt, and a bottle of Saint Michael oil. I have no idea who blessed that water, by the way. It might have been blessed by some guy named Wayne for all I know. The Saint Michael oil might have been blessed by a guy named Mike. (Mike might have blessed the salt, too. I'm clearly not picky about this shit.)

We arrive at their pad with hugs all around and are greeted by their sweet little pooch; then I begin to scope the place out. My trusty assistant/wife holds my stuff and hands me things as I need them, bless her heart. Suzanne is always supportive and rolls with my punches. She laughs at my quirks. She loved me when we first met despite my raggedy jean shorts, permed hair, bright-red lipstick, and penny loafers held together with duct tape (because this Okie didn't know at the time that you could actually get your soles replaced). She might be "light and airy," like Roxane said, but she is still the string to my balloon.

I start in Alex and Dawn's office, and all goes well. I really don't talk much when I'm doing my thing, just recite the Lord's Prayer over and over as I perform my house-clearing ritual. We work through the office, then to another spare bedroom, making our way counterclockwise.

Finally we get to a guest bathroom, and that's when it happens: I cannot retrieve a single word of the Lord's Prayer to save my life. At one point I actually lose my equilibrium and start to teeter—and I am not a teeterer. I have gravity on my side with my short legs strapped to flip-flops. I simply do not teeter—ever. But now I'm so thrown off that I lose my balance, bump into Suzanne, and almost knock her over.

"What the fuck is going on in this bathroom?" I ask.

"Well, our dog really doesn't like to come in here," Dawn replies a bit sheepishly.

*No shit*, I think. I wouldn't like to come in here, either. The air is so heavy it takes my breath away. Whatever's lingering in the room sucks big time and I need to get it out of here. Mind you, I don't really know what "it" might be; remember, there's no instruction manual for what I'm doing.

"Baby, get my bag," I say to Suzanne.

"Okay, honey," she replies.

She comes back with my bag, and I home in on the ceiling vent, flicking holy water toward it; then I toss around the blessed-by-Wayne salt. I'm making quite a mess at this point, but no one seems to care, which makes me wonder.

"So, Alex, what aren't you telling me about this bathroom?" I ask.

"Well, um, every evening when we come home, the bathroom door is closed and sometimes locked. And, well, it's open every day before we go to work."

"Really? You didn't think that was an important detail to share?"

"Well, we just wanted to see if you would find it. We didn't know if you were the real deal or not." He looks both embarrassed and seriously spooked.

Fair enough, I guess, but *fuck you* ran through my head. I turn to his wife.

"Okay. Delta Dawn." That's what Suzanne and I call Dawn; sadly she and Alex are too young to get the Tanya Tucker reference. "Will you please get me a small bowl, preferably a ceramic one?"

Delta Dawn comes back with an oil-and-vinegar dipping bowl.

"You know that this is your bowl's resting place. This will be its last use," I warn her.

"What do you mean?" she asks.

"What I mean is that I'm going to put the whole bottle of Saint Michael oil in this bowl and leave it here by the sink. You'll know when it's time to get rid of it, but don't pour it down your drain. Take it outside and bury it in the ground, bowl and all. Mother Nature will take care of this little bastard."

Honestly, I have no idea what I am saying. I'm not even sure that these words are coming out of my mouth (except for "little bastard"). I feel like I'm being guided.

We leave the bathroom and make our way around the rest of their condo, then head for a restaurant, down a few cocktails, and talk for hours. How fucking crazy was that experience? I ask. And why the fuck did you *not* want to investigate the invisible shit going on before I came on the scene for your bathroom makeover?

✂━✂

Eventually I come to understand that my relationship with Alex is not coincidental. Not enough time has passed as friends to explain our mutual love and admiration for one another, but energetically it makes total sense. I begin to understand that Alex's testing of my ghost-hunting skills, though he no doubt didn't recognize it consciously, was a service to my soul; he was doing me a favor by not telling me in advance what they were encountering in their guest bathroom.

You're probably wondering what happened afterward with the ghost activity in their bathroom. Well, it stopped that day and never happened again. One day Delta Dawn felt it was time to dispose of the Saint Michael oil and she did so as instructed. Maybe one day I should get Julie the Evil Ghost Slayer printed on a V-neck T-shirt. (And yes, I *am* specifying V-neck because I hate crewnecks; they make me look like I don't have a neck, and men who don't pay attention call me "sir." That's why I broke up with crew necks in 2011—some guy called me "sir" at a San Diego

Chargers game. Fuck that guy. I will retract Alex's fuck and give it to that guy at the Chargers game.)

The experience in Alex's condo isn't the only thing that ties me to him, however; our ties went deeper and darker, in surprising ways. What is clear by then, however, is that I've reconnected to the power of prayer in a way that I never experienced before.

So I keep on with my house clearing and my prayers, hauling my tool kit around everywhere I go. I'm on a mission like some sort of hobbit hell-bent on house clearing every corner of Middle Earth. "An elf's works is never done," Brenda tells me. And she's right.

# CHAPTER THIRTEEN

# Jack of All Clairs

> *Time's not a line. It's a circle or a figure eight
> or a goddamn Slinky. If you can believe that, I
> don't know why you can't believe that someone
> might be able to glimpse something farther along
> the Slinky.*
>
> —MAGGIE STIEFVATER, *THE DREAM THIEVES*

The deeper I trek into the cosmic wilderness, the more intensely I start to experience senses called "clairs" that introduce me to even stranger corners of our universe. Before I began my ghost photography, I thought that Clair was a popular girl's name or a place to buy crappy bangles at the mall. I didn't realize that the term was used to define the multitude of senses we possess beyond our sixth sense. What I *did* know by this time is that when one door opens in life (in this case, my ghost photography), another door opens, and sometimes a wall gets knocked down or the roof blows off.

The *Oxford English Dictionary* defines our sixth sense this way: "A supposed intuitive faculty by which a person or animal perceives facts and regulates action without the direct use of any of the five senses." This sixth sense is the general category that houses all our clair abilities.

The "Abcderium of Extra/Sensory Powers" (sixthsensereader .org) explains the origin of the clair naming system. "The English-language prefix 'clair-,' from the French 'clair(e),' meaning 'clear,' when coupled with a root associated with a conventionally recognized sense-ability, generally implies some extraordinary or super-sensory extension or 'doubling' of such abilities in a mode which exceeds limits to the availability of sense-data inherent in conventional understandings. Examples include *clairvoyance* ('clear seeing')."

The most well-known clair is certainly *clairvoyance*, which literally means "clear-sighted" in French. It wasn't until the mid–nineteenth century that we attributed to it the meaning of having psychic or supernatural abilities beyond our normal five senses, including the ability to intuit future events before they happen. But there are other types of clairs. In fact, there are enough of them to fill a baseball roster.

Here are the clairs at a glance:

* *Clairvoyance* is the ability to see psychic energy as words, colors, visions, videos, or pictures.
* *Clairaudience* is the ability to hear psychic energy as words and sounds.
* *Clairsentience* is the ability to feel or sense psychic energy in your physical body and translate it to messages.
* *Claircognizance* is the psychic ability to know information without the prior knowledge or experience. This shares a common border with precognition, or the ability to see events before they happen.
* *Clairolfaction* is the psychic ability to smell information that is not in your surroundings.

* *Clairgustance* is the psychic ability to taste information without the substance physically in your mouth.
* *Clairtaction* is the psychic ability to physically feel the act of being touched by a spiritual being.
* *Clairtangency* is the psychic ability to hold an object or touch another person and know information or history about the object or person.
* *Clairempathy* is the psychic ability to experience another person's emotional state, goals, intentions, and even physical pain.

There are incredible contemporary überpsychics like Brenda who've experienced many or all of these clairs, and historical heavy hitters like Joan of Arc, for example. She was an unassuming French woman who no doubt had many clairvoyant senses, but her clairaudience went down in history like no other—and stirred up a lot of shit.

"My voices tell me I must go against the English," Joan famously said, and then she did just that. These voices, which Joan said came from various archangels, compelled her to drive legions into battle against the English in the fifteenth century. Like countless women (and a couple of guys) who seriously messed with the rigid belief systems of their times, Joan ended up burned at the stake, though she was later canonized as a saint—and went on to become the subject of movies and countless books. Not surprisingly, modern science has suggested that her clairvoyance and clairaudience resulted from migraines, among other neurological afflictions. I don't know about you, but the very idea of driving legions into battle against hairy, warring Anglo-Saxons is enough to *give* most people a migraine.

Joan of Arc, of course, is not alone in the constellation of stars who've gone down in history for their incredible clairvoyance. Nostradamus combined astrology with clairvoyance and is perhaps second to Joan of Arc in his enduring celebrity status. Also French, Nostradamus came on the scene roughly a century after Joan of Arc with his *Les Prophéties*—prophecies that foresaw major world events and are among the most hotly contested and passionately read documents of our time. (Nostradamus's work continues to be published to this day.)

Twentieth-century American mystic clairvoyant Edgar Cayce is considered, more recently, a prophet and the founder of spiritualism and the New Age movement. Like Joan, Cayce discovered his gifts as a young boy when he heard voices and got in touch with both his amazing claircognizance *and* his clairvoyance. But there are other, lesser-known individuals who were also clairvoyant or precognizant. Mark Twain had a prophetic dream that foresaw the death of his brother; Abraham Lincoln was deeply involved in the spiritualist movement (his precognitive and clairvoyant abilities are well documented); and even George Washington and Ben Franklin experienced various clairs and/or were deeply interested in spiritualism, mysticism, and clairvoyance. Then there are the untold number of people today who experience various clairs (but haven't come out of the spiritual closet), and all the celebs who see psychics on a regular basis, never mind political figures (think Winston Churchill, among others) and law enforcement officials who've consulted clairvoyants to help them unravel complicated cases.

~~~

As with anything in life, we excel at some things and aren't so great at others. Throughout my life I've been a kickass golfer, basketball player, softball player (OMG, I'm such a lesbian), and bowler. But I'm a terrible gymnast and horseback rider—not my thing. The same principle holds true with the clairs. I've experienced a number of these different clairs, which I'll explore as we move through these pages. For now, I think it's worth addressing just a few.

Let's start with what you may have seen on TV from one of the kindest souls on the planet: Tyler Henry, from the series *Hollywood Medium*. Tyler has the gift of clairvoyance and clairtangency (also known as psychometry), which is the ability to get information about a person from either an object they wear with regularity (a ring or a necklace, for example) or one that's precious to them. Many psychics use this as a way to tap into the spiritual energy around an individual. Tyler Henry is quite gifted in this arena and has put it in the cultural spotlight through his TV presence. He and I met in one of the bungalows at the fancy Beverly Hills Hotel because I have a friend at E!. (That's when it pays to work in Hollywood.)

After our polite greeting, I hand him one of my favorite bracelets that belonged to my mom. It has a thick chain with a tiny barrel charm that holds a pair of teeny dice inside. I spent countless hours with this bracelet as a kid lying on the floor of my mom's closet, where she kept her jewelry box. Needless to say, that bracelet holds a tremendous amount of love to me, none of which was previously known to Tyler. Once he held it in his hand, he looked at me and right away said: "Your mom, Margaret, is funny and says she is the reason you started writing your book."

To reiterate, I did not tell him anything in advance—including my mom's name. I was totally blown away. Just that sentence alone was magical to me. For starters, her name is not terribly common these days, and how the hell did he know I was writing a book? I'm here to tell you that Tyler is really good. He's the real deal *and* an utter sweetheart—a very kind and gentle being.

Like other mediums, Tyler might also be somewhat claircognizant. The most dramatic experience I ever had with this clair was when Mona told me about her NDE. To recap, knowledge practically poured into her head while she was considered clinically dead; when she came back to life she was a walking encyclopedia about world religions and various aspects of mysticism that she knew *zero* about beforehand. After Mona's passing I asked her sister Pam about the depth of Mona's religious knowledge. "She didn't know a thing before her NDE," Pam replied. "And God knows she didn't even read more than a menu before she passed away. I can't explain how she knew everything she did."

Pam's not the only one who can't explain it. Science can't explain these accounts of extraordinary knowledge, many of which happen to people without having an NDE. Savants throughout history have possessed extraordinary knowledge and mental abilities that surpass even computers. Daniel Tammet is the subject of a documentary called *The Boy with the Incredible Brain*, in which scientists try to understand how Tammet, by the age of four, was able to perform extremely complicated mathematical calculations to the hundredth decimal in his head (often far surpassing a computer's accuracy) and learn an entire language in a week. (In this case, the ridiculously difficult Icelandic language.)

In the documentary, scientists film Tammet computing crazy-complex equations in his head. While he does so he makes small movements with his fingers on the table as if he were tracing something invisible. When the scientist asks what he's doing with his fingers, Tammet replies: "I'm seeing the numbers—but I'm not seeing them. It's strange. I'm seeing pictures, shapes, and patterns." He goes on to describe an almost psychedelic world made up of shapes, "like a square, the texture of water drops, ripples almost . . . like a bubble with a half-cloud . . . something metallic." As Tammet continues to describe a clairvoyant world of images that symbolize complex knowledge, the narrator-scientist says of Tammet's remarkable gift: "It sounds preposterous, but if it's true, it blows away scientific theory."

Yup. It sure does.

Some people, by the way, believe that claircognizance of this sort is linked to the "Akashic Records." This is a theosophical term that describes a mystical compilation of all the world knowledge ever experienced or computed by human beings and throughout the history of the universe. Edgar Cayce was one of many clairvoyants who has referred to the Akashic Records in the context of various clairs. His enduring organization, Association for Research and Enlightenment, describes the Akashic Records on its website as a "Book of Life" that can "be equated to the universe's super-computer system. It is this system that acts as the central storehouse of all information for every individual who has ever lived upon the earth. More than just a reservoir of events, the Akashic Records contain every deed, word, feeling, thought, and intent that has ever occurred at any time in the history of the world." Maybe Tammet and similar savants are taping into this Etheric Encyclopedia of Everything.

My own experience of claircognizance was far more ordinary: It came through automatic writing. This is sometimes confused with "wild writing" and "stream of consciousness" writing, which, like automatic writing, is a form of writing that involves bypassing your critical mind and allowing something else to guide your hand. Sometimes that "something else" is a creative place that's been hidden deep within; other times it is effectively a conduit for information from higher sources. This is what happened to me one day in the spring of 2017: I was sitting in our living room when, without any conscious foresight, I picked up a pen and paper and did I was "told," so to speak. Here's what my hand wrote:

> *I am in charge of my space, my soul, my body,*
> *my home base.*
> *If you are not here for the highest good of these,*
> *you are cordially invited to leave.*
> *You can go, go away from here.*
> *Never come back, not even near.*
> *If you do not, you will not be gainful.*
> *As I am now calling on my guardian angel.*

I looked back at what I wrote and thought: Where did this come from? What is this? A poem? A mantra? A prayer? It felt like a gift, this flash of words on the page. I recall thinking how powerful it would be if every kid around the world had these words for spiritual protection. The instant inspiration and flow of those words that came seemingly out of the blue reminds me of how Jeff Somers describes J. R. R. Tolkien's experience writing *The Hobbit* in an article titled "The Fascinating Origin Stories of 7 Famous Novels" on barnesandnoble.com: "It sounds like a made-up story, but it's true: Tolkien, a professor, was grading papers in his office when he happened on a blank sheet of paper and wrote down a sentence that came to him from out of nowhere: 'In a hole in the ground there lived a hobbit.' No one, apparently, was more amazed at the sudden presence of this sentence than Professor Tolkien himself—especially the word *hobbit*. That sort of inspiration and automatic writing is the sort of thing writers live for."

Not only was Tolkien not consciously, logically, or strategically trying to conjure up *The Hobbit*, he didn't even flipping know what the word "hobbit" meant. That word didn't exist until it popped into his head and came to stand for the imaginary small humans with hairy feet we've all come to know and love.

Was Tolkien claircognizant? Are many artists claircognizant in their own ways? You decide. One thing is certain: It pays to listen carefully to your intuition, because it shares airspace with whatever inspires claircognizance—that sudden flash of insight or clarity, an "aha!" moment or that subtle feeling or "knowing-ness" about something or someone you can't describe but know is right. Here's what I have to say about your intuition and inner voice: Pay attention to them. Always, always pay attention.

*One thing is certain: It pays to listen carefully to your intuition, because it shares airspace with whatever inspires claircognizance—that sudden flash of insight or clarity, an "aha!" moment or that subtle feeling or "knowingness" about something or someone you can't describe but know is right. Here's what I have to say about your intuition and inner voice: Pay attention to them. Always, always pay attention.*

꙳ ～ ꙳

Clairempathy is another clair that I've experienced—I was born into it because I've always been deeply sensitive. My crunchy exterior shields a marshmallowy inside. I have a hard time watching the news because the pain of watching suffering is often too much for me to handle. Just hearing about injured or mistreated animals brings me to the edge of rage. The same goes for hazing troubled kids (especially those with handicaps) or abusing the elderly. Every single time I am on the side of the abused, never the abuser, no matter who they are or what the circumstances. I learned later that this is a form of clairempathy, and it's the only clair that culls its energy not from the Other Side, but from *this* side: from the living, striving, struggling human side of life.

Now let's not confuse general empathy with clairempathy. Everyone is empathetic to one degree or another, but not all people are clairempathic or empaths. Author of *The Empath's Survival Guide*, Dr. Judith Orloff is one of many experts on this subject that's recently gotten the national attention it deserves.

In *Psychology Today*, Orloff, an empath herself, describes the difference between a highly sensitive person (sometimes referred to by the acronym HSP) and an actual empath. While HSPs have a low threshold for stimulation, need alone time, and tend to be introverts, bona fide empaths, according to Orloff, "take the experience of the highly sensitive person much further: We can sense subtle energy (called shakti or prana in Eastern healing traditions) and actually absorb it from other people and different environments into our own bodies. Highly sensitive people don't typically do that. This capacity allows us to experience the energy around us, including emotions and physical sensations, in extremely deep ways. And so we energetically internalize the feelings and pain of others—and often have trouble distinguishing someone else's discomfort from our own. Also, some empaths have profound spiritual and intuitive experiences—with animals, nature, or their inner guides—which aren't usually associated with highly sensitive people."

Many psychics struggle with those "feelings and pain of others" in their own bodies to the point of being debilitated by them. Until she mastered her own clairs, Theresa Caputo was so overwhelmed by anxiety from these sources that she sometimes wouldn't leave her house. In my own case, I practice a number of rituals to keep me grounded and clear out any negative shit from my house or my own energetic body (see appendix four, "Daily Rituals and Spiritual Self-Care," for more details).

I've always believed that words, of course, are only one form of communication for true empaths. We also communicate through touch, body language, and through nonverbal cues. I always know when I meet another empath, because they always, without fail, declare that I'm the best hugger they've ever met. That's because hugging—and the power of touch—is my dominant humanness. I tend to *feel* communication from the unseen world in my body. These feelings and related emotions automatically translate into words in my head.

⤛⤜

Moving onto stranger turf, I did experience clairtaction and clair-olfaction when I physically felt the weight of a ghost on my body and, weirdly, smelled the scent of a woman from 150 years ago. Before I tell you about these experiences, I'd like to tip my hat to Anthon St Maarten, a psychic medium and intuitive coach who confirmed that the relatively unknown clair of clairolfaction is, in fact, common among psychics and ghost hunters.

"For a long time scientists proposed that our sense of smell is based on the shape of the air-borne molecules that make up different odors," St Maarten says on his website www.anthonst maarten.com. "However, scientist Dr. Luca Turin proposes that our ability to smell may instead be based on how these molecules 'quiver and shake.' Luca believes that the vibrational spectrum of a molecule is the actual property that is detected by the nose, and then interpreted by the brain. In other words, it is possible that our sense of smell is based on vibration, in the same way our ability to see or hear or sense is made possible by our brain's interpretation of different vibrations."

If our sense of smell vibrates like our sight and our hearing, then why wouldn't our nose be psychic, too? Our psychic nose is called "clairolfaction." I met this clair in the fall of 2016 when Ima (the psychic from the Crystal Matrix) thought it would be a good idea to test my psychic abilities in the wild and go on a field trip to a few haunted locations in Los Angeles. She wanted me to learn how to tap into my clairs in the world.

We went to the Banning Residence Museum, a giant house that used to be the home of General Phineas Banning. (Banning was a Civil War veteran, state senator, and known as "The Father of the Port of Los Angeles" for his efforts behind the scenes getting a breakwater and lighthouse built in the area.) After his service in the Civil War, he moved to Los Angeles and built a twenty-three-room house in 1864, where he had five children with two different wives.

The home fell into disrepair over the decades until Phineas's great-granddaughter, Nancy, restored the mansion to its original

Victorian glory, with all the antebellum details of the era (ornate hand-carved furniture, gas lamps, and preplumbing chamber pots). It opened to the public as a museum in 1938.

For five bucks each we joined a small tour group led by a lovely woman who volunteers at the historic landmark. As we were walking toward the front doors of this big-ass plantation house, Ima said to me: "Keep grounded and pay attention to what you see, hear, and feel." (She never said to pay attention to what I *smell*.)

We walked through a number of rooms: a baby's nursery filled with typical baby stuff that's foreign to a childless lesbian like myself (crib, rocking chair, etc.); a young boy's bedroom decked in plaid with wooden toys; and finally to Phineas's bedroom with its four-poster bed, armoire, and chest of drawers. Standing in the corner near the door while other guests followed the guide, I thought they really could use a few mountain-fresh Glade plug-ins. (The place just smelled *old*.) As that snarky thought crossed my mind, I suddenly smelled something—something familiar: You know that shitty old-lady perfume that makes you gag on an airplane? That pungent, floral odor that makes you want to breathe out of your mouth? Well, that's what I smelled. I started taking big whiffs of each female guest in the crowd like a complete psychopath (I looked like my dog Homer sniffing the air). Unable to identify the odor on anyone, I went back to that corner and there it was again, that awful perfume smell.

That smell kept following me around rooms: upstairs to a ladies' changing room adorned with lace curtains and an ornate vanity, then out to the stagecoach barn. Finally Ima, who also smelled the odor, said, "Julie, clearly this spirit wants to tell you something, so ask it."

After making sure that I was grounded, I did just that. The spirit told me that her name was Rebecca and said she loved her home and didn't want to leave. Of course I'm thinking *Who the fuck is Rebecca?* When I tell Ima her name and what she said, she says that Rebecca was the name of Phineas's first wife, who died in childbirth.

"Holy crap, that's crazy," I replied. "Well, she seems perfectly happy keeping an eye on the place. She must have loved it here."

On the way back to the main house, Ima and I asked our guide if anyone had ever experienced ghosts in the house. She glances from side to side to see if anyone was looking. "Yes, but we're not supposed to talk about it."

"Huh. Well, Rebecca wore some strong fragrance, didn't she?" The guide froze. "Did you see her?"

"No. I smelled her, though."

"One of our other guides said that she smelled a strong perfume in the house yesterday," she replied, all wide-eyed and surprised. "She said it followed her around."

Ima turned to me and nodded with confidence at her pupil. I didn't know about clairolfaction at the time, so I just called this "the smelly clair."

And by the way, since smell and taste are connected, I have to say that though I've never experienced clairgustance (that's the ability to taste something without actually putting into your mouth), that clair sounds glorious to me. Anthon St Maarten also opened my mind to a fascinating purpose of this clair. States St Maarten: "Psychics who work in law enforcement or forensics, for example, benefit greatly from their ability to become aware of the taste of chemicals, drugs, or blood. It often provides clues to how a victim died, or how they were kidnapped or murdered. . . . Clairgustance often also serves to enhance at least one of the other, more prominent psychic senses."

When it comes to clairgustance, the principle of knowing your dominant humanness applies. If taste connects you to the world, like being a chef, then clairgustance is possibly one of your inherent clairs, whether you realize it or not. And if you're sitting in your living room and suddenly taste cherry pie, well, you're clairgustant—and I am officially jealous.

⋙⋯⋘

Finally, I might have to tussle with science about this final clair because it's so "out there." As previously mentioned, clairtaction is the psychic ability to physically feel the act of being touched by a spiritual being. I learned about this term for the first time on the website of a healer, psychic, and author named Emily Matweow, who may have coined the term "taction."

"I chose 'taction' because it is an archaic word defined as 'the act of touching or making contact,'" she writes on her website. Matweow goes on to describe a "telekinetic-like ability" to touch both "physical and etheric entities in such a way that both the recipient and the psychic have awareness of the feeling."

Now I realize that the idea of being touched by an etheric entity—aka a ghost—sounds outlandish. But here's the deal: If ghosts are comprised of etheric energy, and energy has weight, then it stands to reason that clairtaction is quite possible. Here's another reason it's quite possible: because I experienced it myself.

Suzanne and I were in Arkansas for Cubby's wedding one year. We stayed with a good friend named Janet Selby, who lives in this fabulous old house that dates back to 1904. Janet swears she has a ghost in the house and calls it "CA." Get it? CA (see a) ghost? Janet is hilarious.

Anyhow, Janet couldn't wait for me to walk through the house and either confirm or deny the existence of CA. Like a good friend, I obliged.

Since I always travel with my protection kit, I grabbed a stick of palo santo and proceeded to set it aflame. Once it burned enough to produce smoke, I blew out the flame and started to walk though the house saying the Lord's Prayer. Every minute or so I'd ask for CA to show himself. I suddenly sensed that there was something around the front door, but in the end that sense dissipated. I then turned my back to walk toward the kitchen area and *boom!*—I literally felt something jump on my back. It had the same weight as, say, a partially filled backpack with a binder or two inside. I knew immediately that a spirit had landed on my back. Energetically, in my mind, I told it to respect my space and boundaries, to no avail.

Now I know that this sounds freaky and might feed the idea that ghosts and spirits are menacing—and some *are* (more on that later). I knew in my core, however, that this particular spirit was more like a playful labradoodle that jumps around when you tell it to sit. I wasn't scared in the least.

"Janet!" I yelled. "Your damn ghost just jumped on my back."

"What? CA is here? I knew it," she said in her heavy southern accent.

"Yup, and he's not following the rules, either. I'm telling him to get off my damn back. CA has boundary issues," I said with my rediscovered southern accent.

"OMG, he totally does. He messes with my boyfriend all the

time," Janet said, adding, "Did I ever tell you how CA locked Joe in the little room inside the barn? CA actually turned the handle to the lock position."

"Wow," I exclaimed. "I've heard of ghosts moving physical objects. I mean, damn, we all bought it when Patrick Swayze pushed a penny up a door in *Ghost*, so why wouldn't CA be able to turn a lock?" (I mean this ironically, folks.)

Feeling the physical presence of a ghost is not as unusual as we may think, though all of this is hard to prove. That said, it hasn't stopped a team of scientists at the École Polytechnique Fédérale de Lausanne in Switzerland from trying. They developed a "ghost robot experiment" that tried to simulate "conflicting sensory-motor signals" that people might construe as ghostly in an effort to prove, as one of their neuroscientists suggested, that our mind is only playing tricks on our bodies.

Would those same scientists say the same thing about savant Daniel Tammet's mind? If Tammet's mind is playing tricks on his body, then wow, those are some pretty awesome tricks.

There are just as many scientists, by the way, who are pooling their resources to study the possibility of etheric life, rather than refute it. That includes Dr. Julie Beischel, cofounder and director of research at the Arizona-based Windbridge Institute, and one of the few scientists in the United States engaged in full-time empirical research with mediums.

All this to say that there have always been two sides of science. Working with data scientists who all have PhDs, I know for a fact that if your intention is to disprove something, you can always find an algorithm to do so. Likewise, you can find the data to *prove* the very thing you set out to disprove. Science has always straddled these two worlds, though it is increasingly faced with astounding and baffling mysteries that defy every form of empirical logic. This is especially the case with quantum physics and string theory, which is so "out there" it makes spooks jumping on your back seem like child's play.

⤙⤚

Science is a fickle beast. Remember, there was a time when scientists told us that it was healthy to smoke, and that we could lose weight by eating sugar and no fat. Today some scientists are trying to disprove global warming. Please know that I am not trying to debunk the entire scientific profession, but you gotta admit: They're not always right.

So if you've experienced something you know to be true, whatever clair you might think it is, I have three words for you: Believe in yourself. Oh, and I have three more words if you're getting tripped up by scientists who can't accept the possibility of the seemingly impossible: Fuck those nerds.

## Chapter Fourteen

# Jacob Takes the Wheel

Sam: *Molly, you're in danger.*
Oda Mae Brown: *You can't just blurt it out like that!*
   *And quit moving around, because you're starting to*
   *make me dizzy. I'll just tell her in my own way.*
[pause; then]
Oda Mae Brown: *Molly, you in danger, girl.*

—*GHOST*

One May morning in Los Angeles I start my day like any other day. My commute to work is roughly twelve miles. That takes around fifteen minutes without traffic and about five minutes as the crow flies. In the clusterfuck of LA rush hour traffic, however, that fifteen minutes can easily become one hour or more if you have to drive on the notorious 405 freeway.

Before I tell you what happened, let me just say that the 405 is a bitch. She's big ol' girl that defines city life in LA: ten lanes wide in parts with nearly five hundred thousand people driving on her every day. In a recent US Department of Transportation report on the state of our country's roads, the 405 swept the honors as the most traveled freeway in America. So you can imagine how busy it is during rush hours. Traffic on that freeway is so much a part of life in LA that it was spoofed in the *Saturday Night Live* satire

"The Californians": Karina (Kristen Wiig), her lover, Devin (Bill Hader), and her husband, Stuart (Fred Armisen), talk in clichés that revolve around different streets that go on and off the 405. It's hilarious—at least if you live in LA.

But here's the deal: I love my commute despite the traffic. The more traffic, the better, because during my drive I get personal and professional phone time. I can talk as loud as I want and say whatever I want. More than that, because it's a self-contained space where no one can interrupt me, I sometimes have some of my clearest and biggest epiphanies on the road.

At around eight thirty in the morning on this particular day, I call Cubby like I do every day as I'm making my way toward Sepulveda Boulevard.

No answer.

Then I call Mona's sister, Pam, like I also do virtually every day. No answer.

Okay, so then I call Dave, who heads up broadcast buying at our ad agency in New York.

No answer.

Now I'm kinda pissed. Where is everyone? Where is my morning entertainment? Where are my connections? It seems as if everyone in my entourage has mysteriously fallen off the radar.

I finally make it onto the grand dame 405 for a few minutes with only one hand on the wheel when I distinctly hear a male voice.

"Put your other hand on the wheel," the voice says.

So I do. Wait, *who* is talking to me?

"If your phone rings, don't answer," he adds.

Okay, I won't.

"In fact, don't look at it, either."

After five seconds of silence, he says with simple conviction: "There's going to be an accident."

*What?* Where? Shit.

I do everything I'm supposed to do: My hands are placed at ten and two o'clock on the steering wheel. I am alert. In fact, my internal alert mechanism had babies and they are also on high alert. I sit up straight, alternating my glance from left to right, then check my rearview mirror. I do not look at my phone. In less than sixty seconds, the two cars in the lane in front of me collide. Swerving into another lane is not an option for me since I'm boxed in with cars on either side and behind me. There is nowhere to go. I am on the 4-0-fucking-5 freeway during rush hour stuck in my lane when the sedan in front of me crashes into the pickup truck directly in front of it.

I pump on my brakes to signal to cars behind me to slow down.

I slam on my brakes to avoid crashing into the sedan. My handbag and gym bag fly out of the seat and hit the dashboard.

I remember seeing the Wilshire exit.

I get out to make sure everyone is okay. I'm ready to call 911, but not ready to tell them that I'm not involved in the crash because some sort of spirit voice warned me ahead of time. The drivers involved in the crash seem fine, though the front end of the sedan looks like an accordion. It's a small miracle that everyone is relatively unscathed. I realized that had I not been forewarned and on alert for an accident, I would have ended up sandwiched between the car in front of me and the one in back. Make that *crunched* between both cars waiting for that 911 call on my own behalf.

I get back in my car and call Suzanne to recount the event. "So who was it?" she asks. "Who was talking to you? Mona?"

"No, it wasn't Mona."

"You seem so calm," Suz adds. "Why don't you call Patricia? She'll know who it was."

Exiting Santa Monica Boulevard and heading east toward the studio lot, I call Patricia, thinking how strangely prepared I was for that collision. "Hey. So I have a crazy story for you," I say, then proceed to recount the details of my morning commute.

"Wow," she says. "I've never heard such specificity from the Other Side."

"Who do you think it was?"

"Well, Julie, that's what our spirit guides do," she says in a super serious tone. "They're with us from birth and help guide us where they can, or where we let them. You know, they nudge us around. I'm pretty positive it was your spirit guide. Have you ever met yours?"

"No, actually, I have not."

"Well, you have now, honey."

"Wow. It's a good thing he was there. I could have really hurt the woman in the car in front of me."

"Oh no, dear," Patricia clarifies. "It was *your* life he was saving, not that of the woman in front of you."

Oh my God. *My* life? My little life that didn't seem so little anymore?

I arrive at work but don't bother sharing my story. I spend the rest of the day drifting in and out of morning events. On the commute home I call Pam.

"Where were you this morning when I called you?" I ask.

"At home."

"Well, I've got a story for you."

I proceed to recount every second of the morning traffic incident. I wait for a "no way" or "holy crap" or at least a "wow" from Pam when I'm done with my story, but instead I get a long pause. Finally Pam says: "Do you want to hear the other half of your story?"

"Why the hell not?"

"You know how I can fall into a deep depression and not get out of bed?" she asks. *Do* I know? Hell yes, I know. For a few years I was one of the only people she'd talk to after Mona died. "So I had the phone in bed with me," she continues. " And I saw that you were calling this morning, but when I went to grab the phone, my body just froze up, like I was paralyzed. I literally physically could *not* reach for the phone."

Pause. WTF?

"You know," Pam continues, "there has not been a moment in my fifty years where my body did not do what I asked it to. What would have happened if I had answered?"

"I might be dead," I sheepishly reply. I say that in my head at least a hundred times until it dawns on me that this is my biggest, most profound experience of clairaudience: I heard this voice as clear as day. It was palpable, real, and urgent.

In retrospect, I realize that I'd experienced what I can only call divine intervention: The minute I left my house that morning, everything lined up in the universe to prevent me from being distracted on my phone: people didn't answer, and Pam couldn't even move her fucking body to answer my call. The spirits were already orchestrating things to prevent me from having some sort of serious shit go down; they were setting things up in advance. We've all heard incredible tales of people who've had similar experiences that can only be explained this way. That one person who, by a series of seemingly ordinary scheduling mishaps, misses their flight on an airplane that ends up crashing into the ocean; that other person who gets waylaid and ends up not attending a concert where some lunatic opens fire into the crowd; even the one house spared by a violent tornado that swept everything else off their foundations.

In the end, I heard the message from whatever the voice was. I was a benefactor of its counsel from the Other Side. I desperately wanted to know who or what had reached out to me with that warning and orchestrated that series of morning events. For that, I turn to Ima. I tell her about my experience on the 405 and give her Patricia's feedback. She explains how spirits can act as guides or protectors to human beings like yours truly, and are assigned to us at birth.

After pestering her to reconnect me to my spirit guide with a formal introduction, we do a few grounding exercises. By now, these exercises have become a daily practice in my life: I wake up every morning and ground our house through the olive tree we have that I call Oliver. I ground Suzanne and me and our animals. I even ground my car using its muffler as a grounding cord—I kid you not. And I always ground myself before tough meetings at work or in the world at large.

So here I sit quietly with Ima and ground myself in her presence. After a few moments, she finally tells me what to do to meet my guides. And it's so simple I want to cry: "Call for them," she says.

That's right, folks. Call for them. Open your heart and mind for them. Be present for them and they will come.

So that's what I do. I'm quiet for a long time, open and focused inward. After a few minutes, Ima asks what I see in my third eye. And what I "see" in a clear-as-day clairvoyant moment is a man with a full head of white hair and a medium-length white beard. He looks wise and biblical, but not in a hot-Jesus way. (You've got to admit that Jesus is often depicted looking like a hipster on his way to the Burning Man festival.) My guy looks sage and elderly.

Ima then instructs me to ask him his name. His answer comes back very clearly: "Jacob." I sit silently for a few minutes until Ima finally asks what I'm doing.

"I'm saying hi to Jacob," I reply as tears stream down my face. "I'm thanking my spirit guide for saving my life. I'm overwhelmed with gratitude."

The word "gratitude" barely describes how I feel. I imagine the sense of infinite gratitude people experience when a firefighter carries them out of a burning building. I could have been killed. Jacob saved my life. He. Saved. My. Life. I was alerted to an accident and became the one domino that didn't fall, preventing an even more potentially devastating collision. Thanks to Jacob, I have one more day on this precious Earth. I'm on my emotional knees in that moment.

Not long after that fateful introduction, Ima gives me homework: I'm to practice more grounding exercises and get in touch with my other guides (because yeah, we don't have just one). And that's how I meet my wolf guides: In the calm centered space of being grounded at Ima's place, two wolves appear in front of me. One is gray and one is brown. They're majestic and hold the protective energy of guardian dogs, a tribal and primal energy that makes me feel safe.

Interestingly enough, that night when I go home I don't get the usual happy-barky greeting from Homer. He's skittish when I approach him, backing up with his head practically cocked. Clearly he can see or sense my wolf guides, which became a palpable presence the very moment I connected with them. Once I ask them to stand behind me, Homer immediately comes over and nuzzles his head on my leg. Suzanne is, let's just say, shocked.

And now I'm able to summon Jacob. He's my sage, a font of wisdom whom I call on for advice from a higher source. My wolves are also my protectors and guardians, with whom I got in touch with once when I was on the phone with Brenda in my car. In midsentence I heard what sounded like a wolf howling at the moon.

"Brenda, did you hear that?" I asked.

"Hear what, my elf?" she innocently replied.

"Oh come on, quit messin' with my already jacked-up head. You didn't hear a wolf howling?"

"No, I did not. It wasn't meant for me," she clarifies with grace. "It was meant for you."

I now summon my wolves whenever I need any kind of protection. I can even call on them to chase the shit out of dark spirits, and they still make their presence known to me with a howl. They even appeared to me once at a drum circle party at the Crystal Matrix. But meeting Jacob was like meeting an old friend. I now knowingly summon him everywhere and call for him whenever I need him. I feel empowered, at peace, protected. Through my work with Ima I learn that Jacob has never been in a human body before and that not every entity has been in one. Jacob comes to me with a specific name and a shape so I can recognize him. Spirit guides do this so we don't get confused if other spirit guides comes through with guidance from the Other Side.

And it makes sense that Jacob comes to me in the form of an

older bearded dude. I have trust and faith in elders. They know more, right? There's wisdom and power that come with age. If a ten-year-old kid had shown up as my guide, I'd probably be pretty dismissive. Conversely, if I were a ten-year-old kid and some old grandpa showed up as my guide, I'd probably be dismissive, too. But if a cat named Fuzzy Butt (the name of my childhood cat) showed up, I'd pay attention. I'd also really pay attention if an invisible friend my age showed up when I was a kid, which is why it's so common for kids to have imaginary friends until the "real" world starts to jam their psychic antennae.

There are occasional exceptions to that rule, of course. Filmmaker John Waters told his story on *Celebrity Ghost Stories*. He described a night when, camping as a ten-year-old kid, he wandered into the forest and saw a white light suddenly appear in the darkness. It was definitely not a flashlight. At first it had no form, then it coalesced into the face of an older man. "It looked familiar," Waters recounted. "It wasn't hostile and it looked at me with a kind of understanding. I should have been screaming. I don't know why I wasn't completely freaked out by it. I froze and looked at it in wonderment and excitement. I was raised Catholic, so I wondered: Is this a guardian angel? Weirdly, it brought calmness to me."

I'd bet ten thousand pink flamingos and a lot of hair spray that it was his spirit guide. Like me, Waters was empowered after that encounter. "I knew that I wouldn't be frightened of anything ever again," he said. "It was a wonderful lesson for me as a ten-year-old kid. I think it helped me become what I am today. It gave me confidence to go ahead and believe in things: in behavior that I couldn't understand; to be drawn to subject matter that I couldn't understand. I felt safe with that spirit or whatever it was.

It made me feel competent and inside and included in something that I had never felt before that night."

Lucky for Waters he had that experience of the unseen world at a young age—and *trusted* it. He went on to become an unapologetically authentic maverick filmmaker. So here's the good news, folks: Spirits are all over the place. Our guides are by our side, ready to give us information if we only pay attention. In my case, the three clairs of clairvoyance, clairaudience, and clairsentience came together to form a cohesive whole, like the caramel, peanuts, and nougat in a Snickers bar. Eventually, they became the foundation of mediumship skills that would guide my world forever.

# CHAPTER FIFTEEN

# Medium Rare

> *People need hard times and oppression to develop psychic muscles.*
>
> —EMILY DICKINSON

> *If it's the Psychic Network, why do they need a phone number?*
>
> —ROBIN WILLIAMS

Meeting Jacob on the 405 freeway was a seismic event in my life. Until that moment, I'd been bearing witness to the spirit world: house clearing, getting rid of scary ghosts in bathrooms, taking ghost photographs, and plying my trade with crystals and rituals. Now, however, it felt like the universe had knocked on my door without warning. There's no Google calendar invite from the cosmic wilderness. I haven't showered and my hair is a mess, but there's an important unexpected guest at my door and I've got to open it.

And so I do.

What happens when I open that door is this: To my great surprise, I begin to cultivate an ability to connect the spirits of deceased loved ones to *their* loved ones. This ability is like having a new superpower, and it affirms what Brenda told me long ago: When the people we love pass away, they don't pass out of our lives. Grief is inevitable; in fact, it's an essential part of being human, just like death. We all go in and out the same door, but that door, it turns out, is never entirely shut.

In the beginning, this new psychic ability comes to me unexpectedly at first, and in seeming random moments. My first experience with this happens one morning when I'm in my office at the crack of dawn. Seemingly out of the blue, I decide to text Tony Sella, though I have nothing specific in mind to say. Tony is my old boss and the guy who inspired me to tap into my own creativity. He's spent nearly twenty-five years marketing films, and he does so brilliantly and beautifully, crafting marketing stories alongside great filmmakers like Jim Cameron, Ridley Scott, Oliver Stone, and Ang Lee. I think he's won virtually every award for marketing creativity under the sun and has certain brilliant intuitive gifts. (Tony and I both felt the ghost of Charles Schulz one day at the Schulz museum before the release of *The Peanuts Movie*, by the way. I was moved to tears when Tony came up from behind me and whispered in my ear: "I can feel him, too." I thought: *How the fuck did he know why I was crying?* It was an incredible moment—a testimony to our deep bond and to Tony's amazing sensitivity.)

So there I am sitting in my office about to text Tony. I just *know* that I have to text him. I take out my cell phone and start writing as if I'm being guided, not consciously aware of what I'm about to say:

*Me:* Good morning, Tone. I'm sorry you didn't get any sleep last night. But glad your mom was there to keep you company. Love, J.

Note: Tony's mom died decades earlier. As soon as I hit send, I get panicky. What the fuck did I just do? Can I retract what I just texted? I suddenly feel like I've lost a minute in my life to some other energy working through me. I am actually jittery. Within seconds I get a reply:

*Tony:* How did you know? You're freakin' me out. Love, T.

*Me:* Ummm . . . I just knew. I've been told it was rude to get in people's heads, so I'm sorry. But I felt it would be okay. XO, J.

*Tony:* Keep it comin'. I love it. T.

I'm relieved that Tony was so cool with this wild information I'd texted him. And sure enough, "it" keeps coming. Not long after that experience with Tony, I'm driving home one night when I get a strong hit of my friend Rebecca; I can actually *hear* her talking about me, so I call her. The second she picks up her phone, I ask: "Hey, Rebecca, I hear you talking about me. What do you need?"

"Oh my God!" she says. "I was just talking about you to my mother. How did you know?"

I don't know how I knew; I just did. In fact, that moment I "heard" Rebecca she was telling her mother the story of when she and I first met. On that day, I "saw" a woman who looked like her hovering over her left shoulder. "Did you lose your grand-mother?" I asked her, "and did she look a lot like you?"

Rebecca looked back at me flabbergasted. "Yes and yes," she whispered with tears in her eyes. "How did you know?"

"Well, I'm seeing a woman who looks like you just over your left shoulder; your left side is your maternal side, so by standing there she's letting me know that she's your mother's mother."

Rebecca was telling her mother this story months later when I "heard" her talking about me and called her. A few seconds after we start talking, I see her grandmother again, only now she's showing me an image of Rebecca trailing around some sort of raggedy doll or raggedy-ass blanket.

"Sorry if this makes no sense," I say after describing the image.

"No, it makes perfect sense!" she replies. "I had a comfort blanket my entire life—my binky. I only gave it up at my wedding." A pause, then: "Why is my grandmother showing you that?"

"I don't know, honey. It's your message." And I really don't know. What I do know is that the spirits are making house calls through me, and that I've become a vessel or conduit through which Spirit can reach out to the living.

*"I don't know, honey. It's your message." And I really don't know. What I do know is that the spirits are making house calls through me, and that I've become a vessel or conduit through which Spirit can reach out to the living.*

This is clearly the case one day when Suzanne and I are driving to Sedona, Arizona. If you haven't been there, Sedona overlooks one of the most spectacular red rock vistas in the Southwest, one that's the site of what's considered a sacred vortex—i.e., a power spot where concentrated energy is either entering the Earth or being beamed out of it. (The Great Pyramids in Egypt, Machu Picchu in Peru, Stonehenge in England, and Ayers Rock in Australia are a few other power spots on Earth.) This power spot was revered by Native Americans for centuries and is now something of a tourist hot spot. There are spiritual vortex tours, vortex retreats and centers, vortex healing therapies, vortex places of worship, and my favorite: Sedona crystal vortex massages and spa treatments. (And by the way, please don't confuse a vortex with a portal. You cannot get a crystal massage and spa treatment in a portal. Trust me on this.)

It's believed that giant leaps in one's spiritual transformation can occur at these sites. No one ever mentioned to me that giant leaps in one's psychic abilities might happen en route, but as we're driving to Sedona somewhere between Quartzsite and Phoenix, Suzanne mentions something about her sister Sally. Sally died suddenly in 2015 at the age of sixty-two from pneumonia. The family was devastated. Sally was a no-fuss, no-frills schoolteacher and librarian most of her life. She was fun but somber; in many ways nobody really knew the *real* Sally, but I think that every day was a pretty good day for her.

Seconds after Suzanne mentions her name, I see her. I don't "*see*" her, see her" with my eyes, yet my eyes are wide open and there she is, strangely superimposed on my vision in a way that still doesn't obstruct my driving. I guess you could call it multitasking and multiseeing and no, I categorically do *not* recommend doing this in your car. In fact, I would not recommend doing it while doing anything else. I probably should have had a Post-it on my dashboard that said: *Do not channel spirits while in your car or operating heavy machinery.*

But I'm strangely in full possession of my faculties for driving and very clear that I'm not putting anyone in danger. And there's Sally as I drive, looking exactly as I remember her after Suzanne and I met nearly twenty-four years earlier. For a few minutes I just drive and "look" at Sally in my mind's eye. (By the way, I don't know what it is about driving that brings spirits my way. Lucky for me California legislates everything on the roads except talking to spirits while you drive.)

Anyhow, I keep driving for a while, wondering if what I'm "seeing" is real. The last thing you want to do is tell someone, much less your wife, that her departed loved one is talking to you if it's just your mind playing tricks on you. Finally I nod toward Suzanne.

"Honey, would you believe me if I told you that Sally is here?"

"Of course I would."

"Well, Sally is talking to me right now. And I see her. It's weird."

I then tell Suzanne exactly what Sally looks like, from her hair (which had yet to turn gray) to her clothes from the 1990s. And Sally is laughing; in fact, she seems overjoyed to be seen. "The first thing she's saying to me is something about Ari" (Ari is their ten-year-old niece). "She's showing me that she sits next to her while she sleeps. I think she's concerned about her." Sally had deep bonds with all her nieces and nephews and would play endlessly with them. She was a phenomenal aunt.

"Is she saying anything else?"

"I think so. But you know, baby, I'm not a very good medium. This is clearly all new to me." And right then, Sally "says" to me: "No, Julie, you're *not* a good medium."

I share that first comment with Suzanne and we all have a good laugh: me, my wife, and her deceased sister, Sally. After that, a solid two-hour conversation ensues while we're driving through Phoenix heading toward Sedona. Their dad pops in a few times while Sally is squatting in my third eye. (I "see" him in the left corner of my eye, sitting on a bench.) He was a sweet man who makes my girl, Suzanne, cry a little when he appears now.

Every once in a while during this two-hour mediumship marathon, I get quiet for a few minutes and Suzanne asks about Sally: "Is she still there?"

"Yup. She won't leave."

And for the record, I don't ask her to leave, either. I always loved and respected Sally. It's nice to have her spirit with us.

After three incredible days of hiking into vortexes and shopping at every single crystal store in Sedona, it's time to go home. As we're on the road heading toward Palm Springs, another spirit pops by for a visit: a redheaded guy with a great body who wants to talk to Suz. I see-hear-sense him. Suzanne perks up the second I describe him. "Oh my God, honey, is that Phillip?"

Phillip Moore was the love of Suzanne's life, not in the husband-and-wife sense but in a spiritual-connection sense. He died of AIDS-related complications in 1986. "What's he saying?" she asks.

"Well, he's really not saying anything. He's showing me pictures. Who is Ed? Phillip just spelled his name for me with his finger."

"You're kidding? He wants to talk about Ed?"

"Yeah, seems so. Who's Ed, honey?"

"Ed was my boyfriend when Phillip and I were roommates. I told you about him, right?"

"I think so; I just didn't remember that his name was Ed." Suzanne now has the biggest grin on her face.

"He's showing me stuff," I continue. "Actually, he's showing a picture of a sliding glass door," I continue. "I don't know why. I think it's not for me to know. Does a sliding glass door make any sense to you?"

"A sliding glass door? I don't know."

"Well, he keeps showing it to me. I think he wants you to remember something about a sliding glass door."

Suzanne reflects for a moment, then lights up. She proceeds to tell me about the time she lived with Ed and friends in a town house that had a big sliding glass door. In the middle of the night she heard the doorbell ring. "So I went downstairs to the front door, looked through the peephole, and didn't see anybody," she explains. "I went back to bed and minutes later the patio door, which was a sliding door, came crashing down. Some guys were breaking into the condo. Ed got out of bed and chased the guys down the street. The cops said that was a tactic used by burglars to see who's home before they break and enter."

"Wow, that's crazy." I keep getting more images from Phillip, only now it's like he's showing me a little film. I can barely make out activity in what looks like a crappy Walmart throwback from the seventies. I ask him to "zoom in," and am suddenly compelled to put my hand toward my head, as if I'm reaching for the bill of a hat.

Before I can explain this to Suzanne, she shouts: "Hats! Oh my God, hats! We used to spend hours at Goodwill and consignment stores shopping for vintage hats. We had so much fun doing that, just being silly."

"He loves you, honey," I say. "He still does. I can see it on his face."

"I know; I love him, too," Suzanne says with tears rolling down her face. "I really do."

All of a sudden I can feel Phillip receding, tell me that he's going away for a little bit because I need to focus on driving. Sure enough, the traffic outside on the highway around Palm Springs is suddenly maddening; for some reason people are weaving in and out of lanes like their pants are on fire. I don't need another close call like the one on the 405, and realize that it's time to work on this budding mediumship ability. I need to be more intentional with information coming to me from the Other Side. And for that, I turn again to Ima.

For several months, Ima brings me into sessions with her as a medium in training. The goal is teach me to be more in charge of the images and information that come my way; to learn to turn that info on and off, so to speak, while correctly interpreting it. It's about focus and paying attention.

One of the most remarkable sessions in this regard happens with two of Ima's clients: a Hispanic woman and her ten-year-old daughter. After I get quiet and ground myself, I immediately start to see images of the little girl's grandmother. She's cooking, making tortillas and salsa in a kitchen filled with herbs.

"Does this make sense?" I ask the mother.

She nods. "Yes, yes. She cooked all the time and had herbs everywhere, all over her kitchen. She loved herbs."

I get quiet again and close my eyes. The grandmother is here with me again, only now she's writing words on a computer—*backward*. I immediately understand what this means.

"Is your daughter dyslexic?" I ask the mom.

She stares back at me, wide-eyed. "Yes, she is."

Then I turn to the girl and say: "Your grandmother has some advice for you: She wants me to tell you that you're so much better off not using a computer right now; it's better for you to handwrite instead. That way you can see and feel your words as you write them with a pen and pencil and train yourself better, instead of typing on a computer."

"But I really want an iPad," the girl says.

"I know, but guess what, sweetheart? You can get that later. It will be really good for you to write by hand."

The girl looks pensive and the mother appears relieved. I, on the other hand, *am* relieved. I may have dashed a young girl's dreams of early iPad ownership, but the experience comforts me. I went into it a bit insecure, not sure if I'd be able to harness this power. The experience with the mother and daughter confirmed that I had the ability to translate images from complete strangers that would, under ordinary circumstances, baffle me. (I've never dealt with dyslexia, for example; it's just not part of my experience.)

The more I'm able to manage my ability to summon Spirit in the service of others, the closer I get to jumping off the proverbial cliff without help from my psychic posse. In other words, it's time for me to put on my big-girl psychic panties and go out on my own. This turns out to be deeply gratifying, particularly when I can help dear friends make connections with loved ones whom they thought they'd lost forever. This comes home in a big way one day when Suzanne and I go to Watsonville, a small town on the central coast of California, to visit our friends Debby and Joe not long after Joe's mother has passed away. Joe is heartbroken, so Debby asks if I wouldn't mind getting in touch with his mom.

*The more I'm able to manage my ability to*
*summon Spirit in the service of others, the*
*closer I get to jumping off the proverbial cliff*
*without help from my psychic posse. In other*
*words, it's time for me to put on my big-girl*
*psychic panties and go out on my own.*

I sit down, close my eyes, and get grounded. Almost immediately, I see a train set, but not an ordinary one. "I see a sleek-ass train set," I say out loud. "In fact, I see multiple train sets."

I open my eyes again and Joe is staring at me with his mouth open. "We had, like, four or five train sets when I was a kid."

"Okay, well, your mother is letting you know that this is her; she's here." Joe's mother also "tells" me that Joe is carrying around too much emotional baggage that's weighing him down and holding him back in life. The messages and images are now really clear: "Your mom is opening up a trunk of some sort," I tell him. "She wants you to see this trunk and put all of your stuff in it. You don't have to say it out loud. Quietly put the stuff you're carrying around in it, because she's going to take it away from you."

Joe is just sitting there, crying. Meanwhile, I'm so honored to be part of their mother-son reunion. I didn't have kids myself and have lived most of my life not having to be concerned with other people.

More important, I realize in that moment with Joe that Roxane was right: You really *do* have to heal yourself first in order to heal others. I'd go so far as to say that it's a law of nature. Consider the great crystal kingdom: Quartz crystals are actually self-healing. When they break, they grow hundreds and sometimes thousands of tiny triangular crystal points over the broken area. Eventually this broken area is sealed up with new crystal growth, and the crystal becomes a stronger version of its original self. Is that not a metaphor for life?

I'd spent almost five years working through grief after my mother passed and grew in the most surprising ways, despite being broken. In some ways, I grew precisely *because* I was broken. And eventually, I became a self-healed crystal myself. I'm sure that Joe is now a self-healed crystal, too, whether he realizes it or not.

*I'd spent almost five years working through grief after my mother passed and grew in the most surprising ways, despite being broken. In some ways, I grew precisely because I was broken. And eventually, I became a self-healed crystal myself. I'm sure that Joe is now a self-healed crystal, too, whether he realizes it or not.*

# CHAPTER SIXTEEN

# The Invisible Ecosystem

*I've written about superheroes. I've written about
talking ferrets and math geniuses being chased by
madmen. I've written about spies and demon-hunting
soccer moms. I've created an entire world that centers
around a paranormal judicial system.*

—JULIE KENNER

*If we reconstructed human spirituality painstakingly, we
would end up with a magnificent tree whose branches go
in so many directions, yet all trying to touch the heavens.*

—HENRYK SKOLIMOWSKI

*This world spins from the same unseen forces that
twist our hearts.*

—DAVID MITCHELL, *CLOUD ATLAS*

Images evoke emotions the way words used to do. That's why
everyone loves Instagram so much. Spirits understand this, which
is why they often come to us in images and symbols. I'm convinced that's also why they presented themselves to me in the
form of ghost photography.

After meeting Jacob and continuing my studies with my spiritual wolf pack, I learn that there's a sort of invisible ecosystem out there. It's not like the ecosystem here in the physical world; spirits aren't eating others to survive or fucking up the wonderful interconnected universe the way we humans tend to do.

Let me explain by way of an example: In the movie *City of Angels*, one of Brenda's favorite movies, the world is populated by angels who hover around human beings, often in times of distress. Invisible angels provide solace to people everywhere: in libraries and hospitals, in traffic jams and grocery stores. They can hear the constant mental chatter that goes on in the minds of human beings and even choose to become mortal to experience human feelings like love—but they pay a big price for that: They lose their connection to the angelic realm. And the human realm, as we all know too well, is messy and complicated.

That sets the stage of our "star" angel named Seth (Nicolas Cage) and a sexy surgeon named Maggie (Meg Ryan) who fall in love when Maggie "sees" Seth while she tries to save the life of a heart attack victim on an operating table—in vain. When Seth finally makes his presence known to the incredulous Maggie, the following conversation ensues:

*Maggie* (about the guy who died): He should have lived.
*Seth:* He *is* living, just not the way you think.
*Maggie:* I don't believe in that.
*Seth:* Some things are true whether you believe them or not.

*Some things are true whether you believe them or not.* Maybe I should have that printed on my V-neck T-shirt instead of Julie the Evil-Ghost Slayer. That's what Brenda suggested the first time I was grappling with the ghosts showing up in my photos. "I use the example of *City of Angels* all the time," she said, "because it so beautifully illustrates how spooks are everywhere, which is why it's not a big deal to capture one on film. I've been doing it my whole life."

So if we all had eyes to see, what might we see? Well, keeping it simple here, we'd "see" something like an ecosystem. Based on tons of esoteric literature that's been written over the millennia (and continues to be written to this day), here is my take on it.

*So if we all had eyes to see, what might we see? Well, keeping it simple here, we'd "see" something like an ecosystem.*

For the sake of presentation, let's just say that at the top of our ecosystem we find what we call God or Jesus Christ, if you choose to believe. It's where we find the Cosmic Muffin, the Holy Ghost, or Universal Energy. Some cultures use the term Atman, the Spiritual Life Principle of the Universe, the Almighty, Divinity, Yahweh, Supreme Being, Providence, Godhead, the Maker, oh God, oh Lord. I think we can all agree that whatever it is, it deserves a capital letter.

Next on the rung we find archangels like Saint Michael or Saint Uriel. Archangels are like taskmasters vested with the responsibility of dealing with certain shit on earth that we can't get together. Saint Michael is referenced in the Old Testament. When a Jewish friend of mine suggested that Saint Michael would only appear to Catholics, I reminded her that he appears in Judaism, Islam, and Christianity; he also appears in Anglican, Lutheran, and Eastern Orthodox traditions. Basically, Saint Michael is a pretty neutral dude who defends the Supreme Being Out There (hallowed and whoever be thy name) and assists souls at the hour of death. He's also a sort of chief lieutenant charged with keeping dark forces like Satan at bay. You want him on your side. Call Saint Michael and he shall come.

By the way, according to biblical literature, there are seven archangels that correspond to the seven days of the week. This is extremely convenient for the French and other Europeans who always manage to find a saint whose day falls on a Friday so they can have a three-day weekend. Even better is the saint whose day falls on a Thursday. If America is such a Christian country, I often wonder, why don't we have more days off?

If there's anyone who might be considered the first "angel expert," it would have to be nineteenth-century philosopher and esotericist Rudolph Steiner. In *The World of Angels in Man's Astral Body*, Steiner describes angels as "spiritual beings" that work together "with wisdom and set purpose in everything that takes place without our being conscious of it in our bodily sheaths." They've been working on our behalf since ancient Egyptian times and are still hovering around us as we go about our daily lives in our dumb "bodily sheaths."

It's interesting to note that according to Steiner, we humans in our bodily sheaths can only perceive information from angels when we've become clairvoyant. "Conviction of what they are doing can come to us only when we have achieved a certain degree of clairvoyance and are able to perceive what is actually going on in our astral body," he writes. "The Angels form pictures in man's astral body and these pictures are accessible to thinking that has become clairvoyant."

Moving on in our ecosystem, we have our friendly—or not-

so-friendly, depending on the circumstance—ghosts. These spirits were once human beings who stick around the astral plane
for any number of reasons. They might be stuck in a bardo, an
intermediary place between death and rebirth where ghosts lin-
ger sometimes in perpetuity (which is not to be confused with
purgatory).

Our pets are also included in this ecosystem. They bring us
the purest form of unconditional love and emotional support and
never bug us to go to the mall or buy them the latest iPhone. But
what would you say if I told you that in addition to your cat or
dog, the animal world is also present with you in spirit form? Or
that it was time to get in touch with your inner giraffe?

# CHAPTER SEVENTEEN

# Is That a Hawk on Your Head, or Are You Just Having a Bad-Hair Day?

*How it is that animals understand things I do not know, but it is certain that they do understand. Perhaps there is a language which is not made of words and everything in the world understands it. Perhaps there is a soul hidden in everything and it can always speak, without even making a sound, to another soul.*

—FRANCES HODGSON BURNETT

*Maybe it's animalness that will make the world right again: the wisdom of elephants, the enthusiasm of canines, the grace of snakes, the mildness of anteaters. Perhaps being human needs some diluting.*

—CAROL EMSHWILLER

*I've never met an animal I didn't like, and I can't say the same thing about people.*

—DORIS DAY

I love all furry animals (okay, maybe not hairy spiders) and am glad we've finally come around to acknowledging the value of their emotional support, but here's the thing: Animals have been worshipped and idolized forever. It doesn't take much historical sleuthing to find animals revered by everyone from ancient Egyptians and Greeks all the way to present day—and I'm talking about everything from beetles, bats, birds, and baboons to cows, cats, camels, and crocodiles. There's also our Western zodiac with its ram, bull, crab, lion, scorpion, goat, and fish; and there's the Chinese zodiac with its rat, ox, tiger, rabbit, snake, horse, sheep, monkey, rooster, dog, and pig. Native Americans worship bears, whales, and hawks, among other animals. We also associate animals with our football teams and state flags, and incorporate their attributes into our language and habits. Some of us swim like fish, fuck like rabbits (the only time "fuck" has been used as a proper verb in this book), walk at a snail's pace, and are as strong as an ox—not necessarily in that order.

It's a veritable psychic petting zoo out there, so is it really a surprise that spirit animals are as prevalent as guardian angels or spirit guides? That's a rhetorical question, by the way, and I'm going to answer it first by way of another dear friend, Sari Baumann.

*It's a veritable psychic petting zoo out there, so is it really a surprise that spirit animals are as prevalent as guardian angels or spirit guides?*

I met Sari a few years back when she worked as an ad sales executive for E!. We met under circumstances that were not unlike when I met Alex Van Camp. Apparently I have a reputation for being too tough in meetings. I can have a rough exterior that only a few special ones can break through. I could be nicer, I guess, but my inability to suffer fools overpowers any pleasantries I could possibly muster when every sales executive from every media outlet on earth comes knocking at my door.

Sari is one such exec. Our first encounter goes something like this:

A PowerPoint slide comes up on the large screen in the conference room where we're gathered. This particular slide has a rather lofty claim stating that the cable network with whom she is employed reaches an egregiously large percentage of the US population. I think the number is upward of 70 percent.

"I find this hard to believe," I say during her presentation. "In fact, there's no way in hell it can be true. Looks like creative math to me."

Sari takes a long pause, looks straight at me, then responds with this little gem: "Huh. I hear we've been in this position with you before, so before I defend a statement that was devised by someone other than me [their marketing department], let's just say that you're right unless I can personally prove you wrong."

I can't begin to tell you the utter joy I feel when someone shuts me down. I immediately respect her will, guts, and fearless pregnant pause. I want to be her friend.

And so it is. We quickly become friends, and not your ordinary, run-of-the-mill, hang-out-every-once-in-a-while friends. We become very close. Finding out that she's a millennial lesbian is an added bonus, because meeting a sister lesbian in the corporate world is like finding a twin you lost at birth. It doesn't take long before I tell her about my ghost photography. (Only much later does she tell me that she thought ghost crap was hocus-pocus until we met.)

Our bond is anchored in wicked humor, arts and crafts, and various oddities. Our dads have the same birth date, we both manipulated our way out of college foreign language by saying we had a learning disability, and I'm pretty sure she wet the bed until she was twelve, too. I think that qualifies for a check mark in the bonding column, yes?

So our story begins on our first Christmas season as friends. We decide to have dinner together at an Asian fusion restaurant in LA called Rock Sugar. Imagine a huge airy place with high ceilings, giant gold Buddhas, and more of those annoyingly beautiful waiters and waitresses. In any case, this isn't exactly the first place you think of to celebrate Christmas, but you give and take in any relationship. Sari lets me call it our "Christmas exchange," even though she's Jewish. And I agree to eat Asian-fusion food because that's apparently a very Jewish thing to do at Christmas (at least in Los Angeles and New York).

We're excited to exchange Christmas presents, which we've made by hand for each other. Sari is quite gifted at stringing together the perfect beads with the perfect charms for bracelets. She also has an exquisite talent for making Shrinky Dinks—custom-made Shrinky Dinks, by the way, no tracing. They're impressive, I must say. My crafts come in the form of pottery, metal sculpting, and jewelry making.

We barely sit down for five seconds when I place two gift bags on the table and say, "Go head, open."

"Hold on, killer. You gotta give me a minute or two to ac-climate to our new surroundings," Sari says with her trademark sarcasm.

"Okay, fine, you smartass."

I proceed to order for the both of us, which means that I order enough for a family of seven. The dishes keep on coming, from pot stickers to Indian flatbread to green curry to Princess Chicken. (Princess Chicken is code for terribly overpriced but delicious fried chicken swimming in sugar syrup. You can get the same thing at KFC: chicken strips with a packet of honey. That little tidbit just saved you eighteen dollars.)

Finally we exchange gifts. Bracelets, pendants, pottery, and Shrinky Dinks cover the table, which radiates a certain indescrib-able warmth. When you make something for someone, they can feel you in that object. The creator leaves their imprint. To me this is the highest form of generosity.

After surveying our handiwork and gathering the tissue paper scattered on the table, I look up at Sari and feel my left eye squinting. And there I see, perched on Sari's head, a spectral-looking hawk. "Sar," I say. "Don't be alarmed, but I see a hawk on your head."

"Get it off me; I hate birds," Sari replies, shaking her head. She's used to the crazy paranormal-spiritual shit that flies out of my mouth on a daily basis, so she isn't surprised by my com-ment. She's also the only person I know who got attacked by a nonpredatory winged creature at a bird store.

I continue to watch the hawk flap its wings right over her head, a little awestruck. "I can't get it off of you," I say. "I think it's your spirit animal."

"I don't want a hawk to be my spirit animal," she replies

matter-of-factly. "Can't I have something cute and fuzzy? Or a bear? I want a bear."

"Um, not only do I not understand what's happening right now, I'm pretty sure this isn't *Total Request Live*. I know a little somethin' about spirit animals, but this shit is bananas."

"A monkey. I want to be a monkey. Come on, a hawk, really?" Sari replies.

"Oh for God's sake, let's look it up and see what the Internet machine says about having a hawk as a spirit animal. You're driving me batshit."

"How about a bat? Oh wait, I think I'd rather be a hawk. Okay fine. Look it up," Sari finally insists.

I reach into my handbag for my trusty iPhone, wondering if maybe the Princess Chicken is giving me hallucinations. But the hawk is still on her head when I look back at her, wings slowly flapping.

I search online and find a brilliant site called whats-your-sign .com that has an entire lexicon of spirit animals and their significance. In a video on the Internet, founder Avia Venefica describes animal totems or spirit animals as "a representation of an animal, energetically speaking. They're an affinity, an affiliation, or a connection to an animal." Each person has a different animal that, "because of its behaviors, its environment, its proclivities, its attributes," relates and reflects our inner psyche in profound ways. "Animals are of a wild, pure consciousness," says Venefica.

Presumably, if you want to experience certain qualities in your life, you can focus on a particular animal energy: an elephant for patience and wisdom, for example, or a lion for strength.

Here's a taste of what Venefica's site has to say about the hawk, which I share with Sari at the table:

*If the hawk is your totem, you are extremely perceptive. You see things others miss. Your vision goes beyond the physical too— you have a knack for seeing into the souls of people you deal with. You might call it a gift of intuition. You just have a sense, or an "aerial view" into what is going on in the hearts of people.*

It goes on to say that hawk people are honest, loyal, direct, and protective; they're also visionaries and problem solvers who can see the big picture.

We both stare at each other, a bit stunned. "That sounds just like me," Sari finally says.

"I couldn't have described you better if I tried. Welcome to your tribe, my friend. You're a hawk."

Sari replies with: "Cool. My new hashtag is #hawk."

And that's how it starts. Every text from Sari thereafter is signed with #hawk. (Watching Sari text is like watching a master at work. The battery life on her phone is always at 1 percent because it's like another appendage.) From then on, I start seeing people's spirit animals, whether I want to or not. I've seen giraffes, dolphins, bobcats, elephants, owls, badgers, and a whale. At work we have a lizard, an ostrich, and a carp, among others—and yes, we all sign our names with the corresponding animal emoji, except in the case where such an emoticon doesn't exist, like in the case of the platypus.

Before I knew much about a writer friend of mine, I looked at her for a brief moment and got her spirit animal, clear as day.

"You're a platypus," I said.

"A *what?*" she asked. "I don't even know what a platypus is."

"Frankly, I don't even think I've said the word 'platypus' before just now."

A platypus is a duck-billed, beaver-tailed, web-footed, otter-bodied, egg-laying creature that exists only in Australia. *National Geographic* calls it "one of Nature's most unlikely animals . . . a hodgepodge hybrid that hunts by electrolocation."

According to spirit-animals.com, if the platypus is your spirit animal, you "enjoy your solitude and have never really fit into mainstream society. You are comfortable with this because you revel in your own uniqueness and strength of character. You work well on your own, are not afraid to use your imagination and logic to manifest what you desire in life."

My friend looks back at me, dumbfounded. "I'm a damn platypus," she says.

⤛⤜

My ability to divine spirit animals becomes something of a dinner party trick. One night I'm invited to attend a dinner party in Ojai, California, that actually has a topic: "Living the Orgasmic Life." The only dinner parties I've ever been to until then have had one topic: "Eat." They also normally include booze and Cards Against Humanity. (Greatest game ever, by the way. All you have to know is whether your opponents have a sense of humor—or lack thereof—and play your cards strategically.)

I take Sari with me as my plus-one guest because Suzanne is out of town. We finally arrive at the restaurant, greet everyone, and sit down. Each table has a leader who guides a focused discussion at her table about this subject. This one is totally different. When the topic is announced at our table, I think: All righty then, how am I going to get through this? I'm not good at stuff like this. I don't follow rules well, and I drift off on tangents just to stay awake. More important, I'm a bad follower.

A very lovely Australian woman who is not only very lovely but also very thin (Gawd, I hate naturally skinny people; they just piss me off) proceeds to explain why her topic is living an orgasmic life. I think it's a way of asking people what excites them in life. Then she asks the first question for the table: "What gets you off?"

Our skinny leader decides to go clockwise around our table of six (including her). Not only is she skinny with an accent, she is also quite organized. I keep looking at the guy sitting across the table from me and squinting. He's fortysomething, roundish, with a pleasant face. There's something about him that I like a lot but can't put my finger on.

The first woman to answer the "What gets you off?" question admits that nothing right now gets her excited. Fair enough; I dig her honesty. The next guy, who is absolutely sweet, charming, and handsome, gives the answer any straight woman would dream of: "My wife." The next person—the one I'm squinting at—says something, but I can't pay attention because I keep squinting at him. Next up is Sari, who is incredibly uncomfortable. This is not the type of event you find hip, millennial lesbians attending. I think she actually says, "Pass."

Then it's my turn. "So, Julie, what gets you off in your life?" our skinny leader asks.

"Everything," I reply. "Everything gets me off." And that's when I see it: The guy across from me has an octopus swimming around over his head. Naturally since I'm a blurter, I have to blurt it out to him.

"Hey, do you like octopuses?"

"Yeah."

"Well, there's one on your head."

"Cool."

Remember, folks, this is Ojai. Nothing is too woo-woo for these people.

I pull up the characteristics on my phone from whats-your-sign.com and hand it to him. Here's some of what it says:

*Although vastly mobile and quite the traveler, the octopus is primarily a bottom dweller. In symbolic terms this is analogous to being grounded while still having the ability to exist in the watery world of the psyche. It reminds us that we may be spiritual and intuitively gifted; nonetheless, we are physical beings and must temper our psychic gifts with strong foundational grounding.*

The guy continues to read for a few minutes, hands my phone back, and says, "Yeah, that sounds like me."

About a minute later I look at the woman who proclaimed that nothing excites her in her life right now. I squint at her. "What's mine?" she quietly asks.

I stare at her a bit longer with one eye shut. She is clearly uncomfortable. "Oh my word," I finally say. "A pelican—it just swooped down."

This is my first pelican sighting and I'm excited. I didn't know one could have a pelican guide, but why not, right? If you can have a platypus guide, you can certainly have a pelican. I do a quick Google search for "pelican spirit animal" and find spirit-animals.com, then hand my phone over to the lovely woman.

Here's what spirit-animals.com has to say about the pelican:

*Pelican is letting you know that you need to take some time for yourself and go inward. Something in your life is slightly off-kilter and needs to be balanced.*

*Alternatively, this bird also teaches us to take it easy even in the most hectic times of our lives. Make sure to make an effort to float through life and your emotions. Savor each special moment.*

Once the woman finishes reading, she hands my phone back. "Wow," she says. "That is me. How do you do that? Who trained you?"

Uh-oh—somebody finally asked.

I hem and haw for a minute and finally come clean. "Honestly, I have no earthly idea how this happens. I can't control it. I've never even heard of it as a 'gift.' It feels very Native American to me, but I don't have a drop of Native American blood in my body. And no one taught me this or how to perform on command like a show pony. I'm kinda kidding, because I think some people really need this information—something to identify with they can study and connect with."

My new friend chuckles. "I really needed it," she says. "It may just have shown up to help me out of my funk."

Now I don't know what's going on in Miss Pelican's life, but seems this message is exactly what she needs to move ahead and find joy. And frankly, it's not a bad message for all of us. The same is true for Sari's friend Sabrina, whom I meet at Sari's birthday party weeks later and whose spirit animal is also an octopus. Basically, I just looked over at Sabrina and saw an octopus plopped on top of her head, its tentacles writhing around in slow motion.

Sabrina knew of my newly found gift through Sari, so the first thing she says when she sees me staring at her head is: "Is it a panda?"

"Actually, I think you have an octopus on your head." (As I'm talking, all I can think is: *Who* am *I?*)

"Oh my gawd. I have an octopus? Really? I love octopuses. Or is it octopi? Oh my gosh, what does it mean?"

I share what I learned from whats-your-sign.com: "The octopus reminds us to loosen up—relax." (This gets a chuckle from Sabrina's husband.) "Because the octopus can detach a limb at will to distract predators, it has the symbolic ability to cut loose excess baggage in our lives in order to achieve our desires."

This actually goes deep for Sabrina: After she was introduced to her spirit animal, she slowly started to embrace her animal nature by giving up a few addictions she'd been struggling with, what she now calls her "appendages." Isn't it always good to think about what kind of baggage we can give up?

><(((°>

My ability to see animal spirits is the gift that keeps on giving. Sometimes I'll be in a meeting and it literally looks like a zoo or a scene from *Out of Africa*. I refer to those as my *lions, tigers, and bears, oh my!* moments.

During one of my sessions with Ima, I saw a snake twirling around over her head. At first she wasn't terribly thrilled with the idea of a snake on her head; she even looked a little panicked and asked if it was a black snake. Then she wanted to know if it was attached to her. I think she was worried that it represented something slightly demonic, which was not the case, of course. In fact, it made perfect sense that I saw a snake on Ima's head because the snake signifies a healer energy—hence, the symbol of medicine (called the caduceus) that features two snakes and wings.

"So what the hell do you think is going on with me seeing all these animals?" I ask her when we finally get the snake business out of the way.

"I don't know," she replies. "I've never heard of the ability to see spirit animals, but it's really cool."

*Okay, psychic lady,* I think, *you've got to have more than that.* Then Ima does her usual thing: She yawns (to move energy), looks up (I don't know why), and last, starts talking (and not to me). Finally she says: "Remember when you met Jacob, your spirit guide?"

"Yes."

"At that session you also met two of your other guides, your wolves," she adds.

"I did," I respond, waiting for the big reveal.

"I'm being told"—I love when she says that—"that your wolf guides tuned you into that clair. It's part of seeing spirits and part of your mediumship journey."

➤━━◆

So there you have it. The Julie of ten years ago—okay, the Julie of *today*—still can't believe this crazy shit. And guess what? Just when I think it can't get much weirder, well, it *does*.

# CHAPTER EIGHTEEN

# Shades of Extraterrestrial Gray

*It is possible that these millions of suns, along with thousands of millions more we cannot see, make up altogether but a globule of blood or lymph in the veins of an animal, of a minute insect, hatched in a world of whose vastness we can frame no conception, but which nevertheless would itself, in proportion to some other world, be no more than a speck of dust.*

—ANATOLE FRANCE

*There may be aliens in our Milky Way galaxy, and there are billions of other galaxies. The probability is almost certain that there is life somewhere in space.*

—BUZZ ALDRIN

*Perhaps we've never been visited by aliens because they have looked upon Earth and decided there's no sign of intelligent life.*

—NEIL DeGRASSE TYSON

Okay, people, I intentionally put this chapter toward the end of the book because I didn't want to freak you out right off the bat. Yes, it's even weirder than ghosts. And no, I'm not kidding you when I say that I took a picture of an alien from who knows what galaxy.

There. I just wrote it. Interested in reading more?

So here's how this went down. One day I'm engaging in my usual ghost photography hobby/obsession: I've got the sage pots going, Homer the shaman dog is lumbering by my side as I snap pics with my cell phone camera. Later, I zoom in and out of my shots, checking each one carefully to see if there's anything in negative mode. I sometimes add color or change color to better discern certain outlines. And that particular day, lo and behold, I find a hairless creature with giant eyes and a bulbous head. I think: *This is an alien. This is definitely an alien.*

Because my friend Becca is obsessed with my psychic magic and my ghosts—and I love that she's obsessed—I send her the pic. She immediately writes back: "That freaked me out; I deleted it."

"It's just a little alien," I write back. "Don't get all bent out of shape."

I honestly don't think much about it because, frankly, after seeing dancing ghost chickens, nothing surprises me. But one day I mention it to Ima.

"Do you have it with you?" she asks.

"Uhh—does a bear shit in the woods? Of course I do."

I hand her my iPad and Ima looks at the pictures. Then she looks at me, then back at the screen again. "Oh my God," she finally exclaims. "That's a gray."

"A gray what?"

"A gray alien."

I seek clarity: "Okay, what the fuck is a gray alien?"

"They're like scouts," she says. "They come here to observe.

This alien race has a static vibration, which is probably why you were able to take a picture of it." She pauses, then almost gushes: "I've never seen one, in a photograph, that is. This is amazing. It must be fascinated with you."

Well, I've got to say the feeling is mutual.

><

Let me step back and say the obvious: Extraterrestrials might be the only thing that have a stronger vise grip on our collective imagination than ghosts. But there's more of a stigma associated with seeing a UFO or an alien than there is with seeing ghosts, because aliens are not part of our invisible ecosystem. Though they may be able to slip in and out of our dimension (and I'm convinced that's what happened in my case), they are decidedly not human. If they have a spirit or a soul, we can't fathom it. Even people who don't believe in ghosts, for example, have a place in their belief system for their own soul or spirit. Most people don't believe that we are just machines, or meat, or pure biology. Something else animates our emotions, hearts, intuition, and consciousness; some deep pure essence is "us." What that essence truly is has been the source of esoteric and philosophical debate forever.

*Extraterrestrials might be the only thing that have a stronger vise grip on our collective imagination than ghosts. But there's more of a stigma associated with seeing a UFO or an alien than there is with seeing ghosts, because aliens are not part of our invisible ecosystem.*

But the idea that our soul or spirit might exist after death—that it indeed has an afterlife and that our bodies are just a vessel—is familiar to us; it's deeply woven into the human spiritual psyche and narrative. But an extraterrestrial? What exactly is an extraterrestrial?

We can't even begin to imagine any familiarity with this type of creature, though the majority of us believe that they exist, because how could they not when you consider the seemingly infinite number of other galaxies and universes potentially just like ours—never mind those that are infinitely more advanced?

This no doubt explains our absolute obsession with outer space and UFOs, and the countless books, movies, and TV shows that we've created nearly ever year about extraterrestrial life. (Do I even have to mention them? *Star Trek*, *ET*, and *Close Encounters of the Third Kind* are truly just the tip of the iceberg.) In *Look Both Ways*, artist/educator Debbie Millman wrote: "Philosophers and scientists alike believe that if humans can imagine something, there is a distinct possibility that it can be manifested." Yeah, and I'd add that if artists can imagine something beyond our wildest imagination (like gray aliens and time/space warps), chances are pretty high they actually exist.

The international scientific community has been probing the universe for decades for signs of extraterrestrial life, because even though an extraterrestrial is so deeply *not* a part of the human species, if they exist on some level, then we're all intergalactic neighbors. It's quite possible that we're even made from the same particles. That's no doubt what scientist Carl Sagan was getting at when he wrote: "The nitrogen in our DNA, the calcium in our teeth, the iron in our blood, the carbon in our apple pies were made in the interiors of collapsing stars. We are made of star-stuff."

⤝⤞

But okay now, we have telescopes the size of football fields scan-
ning the universe for signs of extraterrestrial life and one simply
showed up in my backyard?

*Really?*

Yeah. Really. I'm pretty fucking convinced of it. So back to
Mr. Gray.

⤝⤞

A gray alien is a prototype of the alien we've re-created in all our
books and movies: He's ET. He and his brethren are the creatures
we've seen in *Close Encounters of the Third Kind*. The first extensively documented case of gray aliens involves a couple named
Betty and Barney Hill, who were abducted by them in 1965. The
Hills went through a battery of exhaustive tests and recounted
fascinating details about how the gray aliens studied them—all of
this is readily available online—so perhaps it's true that they're as
fascinated with us as we are with them.

> *A gray alien is a prototype of the alien we've*
> *re-created in all our books and movies: He's ET.*
> *He and his brethren are the creatures we've seen in*
> Close Encounters of the Third Kind.

Any way you slice it, these short, bald, gray-skinned, long-
limbed, slanty-eyed creatures are mentioned time and again in
abduction experiences and continue to be attributed to extrater-

restrials. It's been suggested that the Egyptian pyramids were designed with the help of aliens (because how else can you explain those massive perfectly aligned triangles?), and that the Nazca lines in Peru were made by extraterrestrials to land their aircraft (because how else can you explain those perfectly straight lines carved deeply into a cliff where you can only—*only*—see them in their entirety from the altitude of an airplane—or an alien spacecraft?), and that extraterrestrials have landed everywhere from Roswell (helloooo, government conspiracy) to your backyard?

Despite all this, I honestly never spent much time thinking about the existence of aliens, much less worried about being abducted by one. It's not that I didn't believe, I'm just not an active member of an "alien club."

But since I've become comfortable talking about my ghost pictures, I start to drop "Yeah, I have a few alien pictures, too," just to see what happens. One night Suzanne and I are at the dinner party of a prominent Hollywood producer and executive. She lives in a beautiful home in a fancy schmancy Los Angeles neighborhood. There are eleven of us altogether, some business colleagues and others lifelong friends of the hostess. After appetizers, chitchat, and watching a television pilot, we all sit down at the dinner table.

The hostess introduces the chef, who talks about the menu and wine pairings. And to be clear, this is not my life. This evening is an exception. The only chef at my house is Suz, and she specializes in Frito chili pie. I'm afraid if those lovely ladies attended a dinner at our home, they would have to all squeeze onto our pet-hair-covered sofa and share a bucket of chicken.

After the menu discussion, everyone is swilling down bottles of wine and carrying on multiple conversations. Somewhere between the soup course and the main course, the hostess decides to take control of her dinner party. She has a very commanding presence; each word is thoughtful and well placed among all the other words she chooses. She tells us the stories behind her beautiful antique dinner table and all the eclectic glasses, dishes, and napkin holders (all exquisite, by the way).

Then without any preamble she says: "Well everyone, Julie is writing a book about ghosts." Then she turns her head and looks over her left shoulder at me. "Julie, why don't you tell us about it?"

I have no problem telling my story about my ghost photography; then I pause, look around the table, and say, "And, well"—slight stutter—"I also have a photo of a gray alien."

A brief silence washes over the table. Finally a guest named Natalie—who appears to be half shit-faced—drops her fork and says, "Okay, okay, I'm gonna say this: I've never said this in my life to anyone, but I'm going to do it now, and you're not going to believe this."

I'm thinking, *Okay, sister, move it along, land the damn plane.*

"When I was in my late teens, me and two of my friends saw"—long pause—"a spaceship."

*Boom.* There it is. Took her a while and a couple of vodkas to get that on the table.

"I have never, ever talked about this to anyone outside of those friends who also saw it," she adds. "We thought people would think we're crazy."

Well, she's right. People do.

I say, "Natalie, may I offer you an explanation?"

"Yes, please."

"Well, try to think about it this way: We live in a multidimensional world. No one really argues with the idea of three dimensions. But sometimes we can enter into another dimension or something from another dimension can sneak into ours. One that isn't familiar to us. Sometimes we feel it and sometimes, like you did, we see it. I've seen some crazy shit with my own eyes. Isn't it possible there are other species or entities that can exist in another dimension? I do think so. And I think that's what you experienced."

While I'm talking, I'm looking out of the corner of my eye at our hostess. Her head is tilted just slightly to the right like when I'm talking to Homer and he has no idea what I'm saying. I think her head tilt is directed at her friend. She's probably wondering why this is the first time she ever heard of her spaceship sighting. In fact, it wasn't until I mentioned Mr. Gray that Cubby's mom, whom I've known almost my entire life, came out with her own spaceship-sighting story. Once people are in a safe space, they reveal all kinds of experiences they otherwise have kept to themselves.

"You're not crazy, and you're not the only one," I tell Natalie. "I have a picture that some might call proof. Think about how a camera takes pictures: They work by capturing depth and dimension. Your eyes can do the same thing."

Natalie looks around, then says: "Yeah, I'm not crazy."

The gray alien, however, is not my only brush with extraterrestrial life. Another one has my head spinning for months.

On July 20, 2014, at 10:44 p.m. PST (everything on my iPhone is date-stamped, which I love), I discover a photo of a creature that I call "little fucker" for months because he's one of a kind—a mystery. I discover him the same way as Mr. Gray: I'm reviewing photos taken in my backyard filled with sage and palo santo smoke when I see a picture of an entity with a block-shaped alien head, no fingers, a squiggly smile, and slanty, deep-set eyes. The following letter and numbers are very clearly delineated on it: C32. No other little ghost pal ever came to me with a message or a code.

I'm completely intrigued, so like any other red-blooded human, I take to Google to see what C32 means. What is this creature trying to tell me? The secrets to the universe? The cure for cancer? That would be magnificent.

C32 first leads me to the library code of a book called *The Collected Works of Abraham Cowley*. I find the used book on a website and a week later it is mine. I never crack it open, though—it's dense and looks incredibly boring—but I do a little research about the old fellow Cowley. Turns out he was born in 1618 and died in 1667. He was an English metaphysical poet (what are the odds of that?) and was once considered the greatest poet of the age. I still haven't read the entire book, by the way. I am blessed with the attention span of a gnat. His lovely book makes a sturdy prop for my phurba, though.

Anyhow, a few months later I dig deeper online and go from Abraham Cowley to a whole litany of things that relate to C32. Here's what my friend Google told me about what the acronyms C32, C 32, or C-32 may refer to:

C-32 highway (Spain): a primary highway in Catalonia
Boeing C-32: a version of the Boeing 757
Caspar C 32: a 1928 German agricultural aircraft
Citroën C32: a van
Douglas C-32: a military designation of the Douglas DC-2

HMS C32: a British C class submarine

New South Wales C32 class locomotive: an Australian railway
    locomotive

Nissan Laurel C32: a model of automobile

Socket C32: a server processor socket by AMD

Bill C-32 (40th Canadian Parliament, 3rd Session): a proposed
    bill that would amend the Copyright Act of Canada

Cancer of the larynx, Internal Statistical Classification of Dis-
    eases and Related Health Problems (ICD-10)

King's Gambit, Encyclopedia of Chess Openings

Caldwell 32: NGC 4631, the Whale Galaxy

Hmmm . . . I went through them all, wondering what this creature might want me to know. Do I have larynx cancer? Should I go to Spain or Australia, several modes of transportation are indicated. Do I need to take up chess? Am I a messenger? Is it?

Crap, it seems like a hard game—does this have anything to do with me at all? Why would a tiny ghost be visiting a lesbian ghost photographer in Sherman Oaks, anyhow?

After a while it hits me: The majority of the C32 acronyms have something to do with a mode of transportation: highway, airplane, van, submarine, locomotive—even a processor socket (which, let's face it, is a sort of mode of transportation for electricity). And that's when the very last entry really stands out: Caldwell 32: NCG 4631, the Whale Galaxy.

Okay, are all roads (and vehicles) leading to the Whale Galaxy? And if so, what the fuck *is* the Whale Galaxy? Surely not some planetary ocean where real orcas live.

Turns out the "Whale Galaxy" is actually a spiral galaxy in the constellation Canes Venatici. (Sounds like a nice Italian restaurant.) According to Wikipedia, this galaxy contains a central starburst that's the site of "intense star formation." So many supernovas have exploded in the center of this galaxy that "they are blowing gas out of the plane of the galaxy." This has created a "superwind" that has "produced a giant, diffuse corona of hot, X-ray-emitting gas around the whole galaxy."

Holy supernova. I'm now quite convinced that that little fucker is an alien. Seeing ghosts is mind-blowing enough, and taking photos of these guys is insane, but an alien ghost? I'm speechless.

I'll never know in my lifetime what invisible ecosystem is truly home to extraterrestrials, but I continue to open my doors of perception. But maybe in the end I opened those doors a little too wide, because I'm about to discover that in addition to angels and other blessed entities, unfriendly spirit predators roam our beloved human invisible ecosystem.

# CHAPTER NINETEEN

# Deep, Dark Debbie Downer of the Universe

*Now clear your minds. It knows what scares*
*you. It has from the very beginning. Don't give*
*it any help; it knows too much already.*

—TANGINA BARRONS, *POLTERGEIST*

Some people call him the Devil, Lucifer, or Satan. Others call him the Antichrist or the Son of Perdition. I just call him Ron. (My apologies to the Rons of the world. Most of you are probably really nice guys.)

Let me explain.

Alex and I are having dinner one night. Actually, I don't think we eat much, but we sure do drink a lot. We like to drink together. (I never said that our relationship is healthy.) Before we get too hammered, Alex tells me about a "condition" that he's been dealing with his entire life. "I have this thing called sleep paralysis," he says.

"Uh, what's that?"

Alex shares what's he's read and learned about this condition. "It's kinda weird," he says. "I'm sleeping and it's like I wake up

179

and can't move my body at all, like something dark and dense is pressing down on my body. It's scary as hell. I can be in that state for at least thirty minutes. And it's crazy—I've started reading stories about other people with sleep paralysis, and get this: We all see the same thing—a guy with a hat."

"A guy with a hat?" I look at him with my eyes at half-mast because I've had two cocktails by this point, not because I don't believe him. In fact, I'm paying more attention now.

"Yeah, can you believe it? What a coincidence, right?" he says.

*That's no coincidence, you dipshit*, I think.

He continues: "Did you know that Wes Craven, the guy who created *Nightmare on Elm Street*, has sleep paralysis and based Freddy Kruger on the man with a hat? I mean, the guy I see doesn't exactly look like him—he's just a dark shadow that wears a hat and a long coat—but isn't that cool? You know Freddy Kruger?"

*No, that's not cool, you dipshit*, I think again. "Totally cool," I say. "It's actually fascinating. I immediately see an image of Freddy Kruger and understand the fear you must feel."

"You know, I've been seeing this guy since I was nine years old, and I'm still afraid of him," he says. "Sometimes when I'm in that state of sleep paralysis, I yell for help from Dawn. She says that I'm barely even whispering, even though it feels like I'm screaming. It's not a dream, either. My brain is literally awake."

Until then I'd never heard of this strange sleep condition, but clearly Alex needs help, so I put together a protection pouch filled with black tourmaline and a protection prayer and give it to him with a handwritten set of simple instructions that read: "Put these on your bedside table and take them with you when you travel. Love, Julie."

A few months go by and Alex gives me the occasional sleep paralysis report. So far so good, until he says one night on the phone, "You're not going to believe this. I'm in Seattle and forgot to bring my rock. Then I had a visitor last night: the hat guy. That's what I get for forgetting my rock."

I give him another piece of black tourmaline the next time I see him—a "roadie," just for travel. In the meantime, I share the story of Alex and his sleep paralysis with Ima, who directs me to an author named Heidi Hollis. Hollis wrote a book called *The Hat Man: The True Stories of Evil Encounters* that describes this sleep-stalking guy with a hat who menaces people, even when they're awake. She also describes a guy who saw the hat man and asked him his name. The hat man's response was, "They call me Scratch."

Scratch, according to the Bible, is a stand-in for the devil who transforms into a serpent, crawls into the abode of Adam and Eve, and lies to them by flattering them away from their allegiance to God. Later, he scratches their names from the Registry of Life. From that time on he's known as "Old Scratch," which, according to Wikipedia, "is a name of the devil, chiefly in southern US English. The name likely continues Middle English *scrat*, the name of a demon or goblin, derived from Old Norse *skratte*."

Okay, now I'm even more curious about the "hat guy," aka "Scratch." So I dig further into the subject and discover that sleep paralysis—and the appearance of a hat guy, an old hag, or "shadow people"—has been documented for centuries. And no one, it seems, has researched the phenomenon more extensively in our day than Dr. David Hufford, a professor and director at the Doctors Kienle Center for Humanistic Medicine at the Penn State College of Medicine and author of *The Terror That Comes in the Night: An Experience-Centered Study of Supernatural Assault Traditions.*

Hufford has a website dedicated to the subject called, naturally, sleepparalysisworld.com. It documents from a scientific and paranormal perspective the experiences of people who describe "a presence of a supernatural malevolent being" that immobilizes them during sleep. This "being" or "shadow person" shares certain characteristics in cultures all over the world. Get a load of Hufford's list of those shared traits:

Malelike, though gender is not obvious.
Could be female in nature, but no race.
Usually very tall.
Usually seen in a trench coat/cloak, or old-fashioned overcoat.
The "hat shadow man" usually has a big hat.
3-D in shape or opaque.
No eyes, though occasionally red eyes have been reported.
Fast, almost like lightning speed.
Usually very silent.
Seems to have mass.
Seems to be able to defy common laws of physics (e.g., can
    move through walls).
Can look spiritlike/demonic.

When I say people all over the world experience sleep paralysis, that's an understatement. "They have been called angels, demons, incubi, werewolves, hags, ghosts, fairies, djinns, aliens and more," author Kat Duff writes in *The Secret Life of Sleep*. In Scandinavian cultures, sleep paralysis is thought to be "caused by a mare, a supernatural creature" that sits on people's chests while they're sleeping. In Africa, this creature is referred to as "the Devil on your back." In the southern United States, it's an entity engaged in nocturnal "witch riding." In China, it's "a ghost pressing on body," and in Sardinia this spirit/demon wears seven red caps. In Mexico, it's considered the spirit of a dead person, and in Brazil, it's a freaky old hag who lives on people's rooftops waiting to step on their chests and pin them down while they're asleep. It's a "shaman of the black" in Mongolia and Shaitan, or simply "Satan," in Urdu.

You get the picture: This shadow presence is a world traveler with unlimited frequent flyer miles and access to the cockpit of everyone's psyche. Instead of going the biblical route and calling this mystery force the Devil, how about we cast a wider net and just call it the deep, dark Debbie Downer of the universe?

*This shadow presence is a world traveler with unlimited frequent flyer miles and access to the cockpit of everyone's psyche.*

<hr>

Duff's book, by the way, is a brilliant exploration of the landscape of sleep. In her reflections on sleep paralysis, she tells us that Charles Dickens (a big-time insomniac) gave the ghost of Marley in *A Christmas Carol* all the telltale features of a sleep paralysis visitation, and he also evoked it in *The Adventures of Oliver Twist*. (Dickens was interested in the paranormal and an early member of the Ghost Club, a British organization founded in 1862 dedicated to paranormal investigation. The club still meets every month in London.)

While Duff offers scientific theories for this "sensed presence," quoting neurologists and neuropsychiatrists, she herself concludes that all the brain research "does not prove that disembodied spirits do not exist, just as the fact that dream intrusion into waking life can produce the sensations of being crushed does not prove that menacing visitations could not occur at the edges of sleep. . . . Perhaps these beings, if we can call them that, are always around, but we are only able to sense their presence when we are slipping between states of consciousness. Maybe they coalesce or come into being under the extraordinary conditions of near sleep."

Maybe indeed.

Hufford goes even further, writing: "Scientists are open to the possibility of other dimensions out there. The majority of [sleep paralysis] sufferers support theories about dimensions and believe that Shadow People have either found a way to enter into our dimension or have accidentally slipped into 'our side.'"

Hmmm, maybe "Shadow People" aren't the only ones who've "found a way to enter into our dimension."

---

So now I am truly fascinated by this subject and call Alex to share what I learned from all this research. "Hey, Alex," I say. "So you know that guy with a hat who scares the shit out of you during sleep paralysis? Well, he's a deep, dark Debbie Downer of the universe."

"He's *what*?" Alex replies.

There's a long pause because Alex can't speak—so I do. I explain what I've learned about this dark spirit and, in total warrior mode, suggest that we get rid of this fucker. "Here's what you do," I say, "The next time that son of a bitch shows up, invoke God or Saint Michael. You choose what greater power you want to invoke, but bring one of them in. And while you're at it, protect your son. Every night stand over his crib and recite the Lord's Prayer or your own protection prayer. Do it with commitment and conviction. It's your job to protect him."

"Wow, okay, I will," Alex replies. He's quiet for a moment, then adds: "But I kinda want to see him again now that I know who he is. What if *you* see him now?"

"Don't worry, I won't. He's not invited. Trust me on this." I say this very matter-of-factly (and very bossy).

Around six months go by, during which time I encounter a bunch of other people who have sleep paralysis: friends and colleagues, daughters of associates. It's like being pregnant and suddenly seeing strollers all over the place where before you saw none. Like Alex, all of these people need protection and spiritual rituals.

Then one day out of the blue Alex calls me from New York. "So . . ." Long pause. "I experienced sleep paralysis again."

"Oh no, you did? What happened?"

"This time was different. I saw a guy, but it wasn't the hat man. This guy didn't have a hat, but he spoke to me. Actually, he laughed first, then spoke to me."

"Well, let's call him the hatless man now," I add, thinking I'm being funny. "What did he say?" I'm dying to know and, of course, I'm thinking he called himself Scratch. But what comes out of Alex's mouth is the last thing on earth I thought I would hear.

"He said, 'Tell her that my name is Ron.'"

I freeze. I literally freeze. Every cell in my body feels like it's bristled. I can deal with ghosts and aliens, but there is only one word that is still a trigger for me. And that word is "Ron."

"Hello? Are you still on the line?" Alex asks. "So why would he say, 'Tell her that my name is Ron'?"

>~~~<

For the answer to that question, dear reader, we have to travel back in time to a sunny day in 1982 in Tulsa, Oklahoma. I've just become runner-up in the state golf championship and am in a state of bliss. It doesn't matter that I lost. I am twelve years old and just set a record for the youngest ever to finish runner-up. And I am quite a vision, too: Nike tennis shoes, shaggy hair, brandishing a three iron from the tee box. I'm a misfit among the proper golfers, and it's this misfit's day to shine. Local television stations and the *Tulsa World* newspaper interview me.

After the interviewing hoopla is over, Mom and I head toward our wood-paneled station wagon. We're joined by Ron, my stepfather: tall, chunky, dark hair, big-ass sideburns, and reeking of Aramis men's cologne.

When we get to the car, Mom decides that she wants to visit the ladies' room before we start our ninety-minute journey back home. With a giant smile on my face I put my clubs in the car, change shoes, then hop into the backseat. Ron proceeds to get in the passenger side of the car. Then all of a sudden he turns around and backhands me so hard across the face that I slump over like I got hit by a frying pan.

"Why did you tell that reporter your dad's name was Tom Rieger?" he asks.

"Because it is," I reply.

"I have had to put up with you all these years; the least you could do is give me some credit," he shoots back.

I just lie there in the backseat, alone with my abuser, feeling scared and strangely guilty. This moment of glory, one of the greatest moments of celebration in my young life, is suddenly killed. Darkness has irrevocably extinguished the light.

Mom comes back from the clubhouse and hops in, so proud of her daughter. She proclaims that we stop somewhere special for lunch and celebrate. To which I reply: "It's okay, Mom, we can just go home."

I don't feel much like celebrating. I won't feel much like celebrating for many, many years to come.

>><><

Why didn't I tell my mom about Ron, my abuser? Why didn't I tell her about the horrors I suffered for years under the hands of this asshole? I've been asking myself that very question for an awfully long time. The answers can—and do—fill countless books on the psychology of abuse. They're also a familiar part of an ongoing tale about male dominance that's been part of our culture for millennia and still makes headlines today. (My #MeToo moment happened decades ago.) But here's the short version: In my twelve-year-old mind, I thought that if I told my mom about Ron, he would kill me or my mom—or both of us.

You're probably wondering where my mom was during his abuse. Well, she was often on the road for work traveling around Oklahoma and Kansas. That's when my abuser would strike. Sitting in the kitchen one night when Mom was away, he ordered me to move the television set where he could see it better from the living room. I did as he wished, with an attitude. This pissed him off, so he picked up the glass saltshaker, threw it at me, and hit me smack-dab between my eyes. He was a good shot, too. I still have the scar on my forehead.

Another time we were unpacking my grandmother's shell art (sounds hideous, but it was cool) when I stubbed my toe on a wood frame—and that SOB laughed at me. Under my breath I whispered "asshole." He heard me and ended up chasing me into my bedroom. The (not) funny thing is that I knew exactly what to do: I knew that if I dove facedown onto my bed, he'd only have access to my back and I could protect my face and vital organs. The bruises he inflicted on my body remained for a good two weeks.

This kind of abuse, large and small, went on for years. However, there was one beating that hurt the most and lodged itself deep into my psyche, and it wasn't even physical. It didn't happen on a holiday or a birthday. Just a day when I stayed home from school with a sinus infection.

It's dinnertime and Ron says, "Julie, get your fat ass up out of that chair and set the table."

I stare at him for a brief moment, planning my next move. Then I proceed to get my fat ass up out of the chair and set the dinner table. There are four of us in the household—Mom; Ron; my brother, Tom; and myself. I set the table for three.

The next move is probably the most pivotal and courageous move I've ever made in my life: After setting that table, I turn around, walk out of the kitchen, and head out of the house toward the street. I have no plan, just pain. I stand at the end of our driveway, look both ways, then decide to walk left toward the railroad tracks and make my way to my friend Reese's house.

Ten steps into my great escape, I hear my mom yelling. My mom doesn't yell. She keeps her cool all the time; she is always in charge. I can't make out what she is yelling about, but I keep walking. Clearly she's aware of the exchange that happened in the kitchen.

I'm scared to death, though there has always been a part of me that is warriorlike. I'm never a bully. I hate bullies. I always have and still do stand up for those being bullied. I guess you could say that I bully the bullies. I can thank Ron for that. In that moment decades ago, I ponder marching back into the house to apologize for being disrespectful.

But I don't.

I keep walking.

I make it about four houses down when I hear a door slam and a car engine start. *Oh shit,* I think. *It's Mom.* I know the sound of that blue 1981 Toyota hatchback anywhere.

She pulls up next to me and waves me into the car. I get in, begrudgingly. I don't look at her out of fear and disgust for her having married Ron. She drives over the railroad tracks to a shitty suburb in our shitty town. Everything feels shitty in that moment. Fifteen minutes into the drive, it dawns on me where she's going: toward the batting cages.

Once we get there, Mom hands me a bat and a stack of quarters for the automatic pitching machine. Then she sits on a bench, just watching me. I can't begin to imagine what's going through her head. About an hour goes by, during which I hit each consecutive ball harder, imagining that it's Ron's head. Finally I'm tired (remember I have a sinus infection) and out of quarters. We get back into the car and head home.

Not a word is spoken from the time she motioned me into the car to when we return home. I look around as we walk into the house.

"Where's Ron?" I ask.

"He's gone," she replies matter-of-factly.

Later I figure out that at the batting cages she was not only giving me an opportunity to vent, she was stalling me long enough for Ron to pack his crap and get out of the house.

I didn't see Ron again after that night until twenty-eight years later, at my mom's memorial. I realize now that what I did that night was save myself. I took a stand in order to survive. I didn't tell my mom the full breadth of the abuse I suffered from Ron, either, until years after that fateful night. I internalized the abuse for so very long. Ron became code for my weakness, which took me years to work through. The word "Ron" became my kryptonite, the one thing in this world that emotionally could bring me to my knees.

Now here's this "hat man" or "shadow person" communicating with Alex and using "Ron" as a foil to prevent me from helping him. How incredibly clever. Whatever this force is—I want to call it the Devil, pure evil—it seems able to draw on people's personal history to scare them. This deep, dark Debbie Downer of the universe isn't channeling Ron (and Ron is still alive as I write this, by the way). No, it's using Ron as a way to obliterate me and distance me from Alex. It had somehow "entered our dimension," as Hufford put it, and "slipped into our side."

Why, though? Why would this entity want to push me from Alex? Here's my short answer: There *are* dark forces out there in the invisible ecosystem, and they're drawn to people not because those people are dark themselves, but because, on the contrary, these people are *light*. And the only thing that can dispel darkness is the light. As inspirational speaker Iyanla Vanzant once put it: "And perhaps you thought, 'Because I'm doing so much spiritual work, I'm only going to attract angels.' No! The more spiritual work you do, the more darkness you attract. Because the light don't need more light. The darkness needs light! The light doesn't need more light."

I firmly believe that this dark force wanted me away from its prey: Alex. It didn't want a lesbian ghost photographer/medium messing around in its turf. It wanted to find my weakest point and bring me down—but that wasn't going to happen.

This was the moment I came to understand in a visceral way that we humans have spiritual power over disembodied spirits precisely because we inhabit bodies. This was when I also understood that this is our essential power, and it can protect us.

*This was the moment I came to understand in a visceral way that we humans have spiritual power over disembodied spirits precisely because we inhabit bodies. This was when I also understood that this is our essential power, and it can protect us.*

✖

I can't diagram this out to Alex on the phone, of course, so my conversation with him is brief. I explain that Ron was my step-father and that the word "asshole" was a nice way of describing him. "Your hat man guy was trying to mess with me through you," I explain. "I knew it the very second you said his name; I felt it throughout my entire body. If there's one word that has the ability to provoke me, it's the name Ron."

"But why would it be trying to get to you through me?" Alex very earnestly asks.

"Because it knows. The hat man guy knows that I'm trying to help you get rid of it, and it doesn't want to leave."

"But *how* does it know?" Alex persists.

"They know everything, Alex."

>~~~<

To date, Alex hasn't seen the hat man again. "The Devil is afraid of me!" I said, laughing, the last time we spoke about this crazy event.

Alex nodded with a "no shit" look on his face. "I don't think I'll see him ever again," he said. "I don't want to."

Guess what? Alex most likely will never see the hat man again; he's protected now. He understands the importance of having spiritual rituals and asserting his human dominance.

This act of protecting ourselves and warding off dark spirits, by the way, is as old as Job. As Duff wrote in her book, "Most cultures provide practices—prayers, amulets, locks, or communal sleeping arrangements—to ward off visitations in the borderland between waking and sleeping, for the nearness of sleep dismantles our daytime defenses, and renders us naked and vulnerable."

*This act of protecting ourselves and*
*warding off dark spirits, by the way, is*
*as old as Job.*

In addition to evoking God and other higher powers, some cultures even suggest telling these spirits where they can go shove it. According to Hufford, a person on the island of Fiji waking up from sleep paralysis "is often asked to immediately curse or chase the spirit of the dead relative, which sometimes involves literally speaking to the spirit and telling him or her to go away or using expletives."

How do you say *fuck off* in Fijian?

✷✷✷

Here's the deal: We don't have to be "naked and vulnerable," but we are all indeed connected—we're connected to the light and to the dark, because we're part of the invisible ecosystem whether we believe it or not.

> *We don't have to be "naked and vulnerable," but we are all indeed connected—we're connected to the light and to the dark, because we're part of the invisible ecosystem whether we believe it or not.*

An article on Lifetrainings.com called "The New Science: We Are Made of Energy, Not Matter" describes the world of quantum physics; how we're made of atoms, and how atoms are made of energy waves. When atoms collide, it's not their "matter" that meets. "What [quantum physicists] see is that when two atomic waves meet, they either meet in synch, creating a constructive or harmonious effect, or they meet out of synch, creating a destructive effect in which they annul each other."

The same thing happens with people and spirits because we, too, are all created of atomic energy waves. And "because it is impossible to separate waves, the new science says . . . [that] we are all connected—our waves are always meeting and getting entangled in each other." It's from this "entanglement" that we can feel good or bad vibes; that we're "magnetically attracted" to someone or instantly repulsed.

Either way you slice this cosmic pie, there's no denying that we're all invisibly "entangled" in good and bad ways. When it's bad, it can be very, *very* bad. But when it's good, well, it can be as good as a damn Pop-Tart.

And I mean that literally.

# CHAPTER TWENTY

# Pop-Tarts

> *An invisible thread connects those who are*
> *destined to meet, regardless of time, place, and*
> *circumstance. The thread may stretch or tangle*
> *but it will never break.*
>
> —ANCIENT CHINESE PROVERB

Not long after my mom dies, I have dinner with the brilliant Theresa Caputo, aka the Long Island Medium. She's in town for a small dinner hosted by TLC as part of their upfront presentation to the advertising community. I'm invited because the TLC folks knew how much I love her show. Needless to say, I'm ecstatic to meet her.

Suzanne and I arrive early at the fancy Italian restaurant in Santa Monica and watch Theresa arrive outside as guests start to roll in. To my surprise, as soon as she walks through the door she comes right up to me, chewing the side of her lip. "Hi, I'm Theresa," she says, extending her hand for a proper lady hand-shake.

I grab her hand. "I'm Julie," I politely reply. "So nice to meet you."

"So, Julie, did you recently lose your mom?"

"I did, yes." I should be surprised by her greeting, but, hey, this is the Long Island Medium I'm talking to.

"Let me tell you something," she continues. "You mom's been bugging me since we pulled up out front. She's a funny one, your mom. The first thing she said was, 'My daughter is so excited to meet you.' Then she went on to tell me that you can do what I do."

"She said *what?*" I think I'm actually turning red with embarrassment.

"Your mom told me and is telling me again right now that you can do what I do."

"Oh, good grief. My mother was the best mom on the planet, Theresa, and she thought I could do anything. One time when I was just fifteen years old she told me that I could do anything a man can do—even better. So I think she's just a proud momma and still thinks that."

"You may be surprised one day, Julie," Theresa says.

>~~~<

Well, yeah, I *was* surprised one day—and I'm still surprised. Theresa Caputo is extraordinarily talented and I'm not nearly in her league, but I am starting to cultivate my own psychic gifts. When my mom passed away, of course, I thought that I'd lost a connection to unconditional love, faith, God, any sense of joy. I thought that I'd live forever with a sense of meaninglessness and profound grief. But I got it all wrong. In the end I gained not only an even greater connection to these things, I was able to transform grief into healing while harnessing superpowers that I never knew existed.

*I thought that I'd lost a connection to unconditional love, faith, God, any sense of joy.*

*I thought that I'd live forever with a sense of meaninglessness and profound grief. But I got it all wrong. In the end I gained not only an even greater connection to these things, I was able to transform grief into healing while harnessing superpowers that I never knew existed.*

I also found peace with the grief of my own life: being an abused kid, having to deal with the challenge of coming out again and again and again—because you never just come out once. Every encounter brings with it the challenge of intuiting how open or closed a person might be. It's a constant dance and struggle.

<hr />

To say that this path through grief was unorthodox is an understatement. I started with the Holy Ghost and ended up with real ghosts, spirit entities, etheric creatures, aliens, and dancing fucking chickens.

You may not believe any of this, or you may only believe parts of it. I wouldn't have believed it had I read this book ten years ago. When something deeply challenges our belief systems, we usually write it off as false because the alternative is to open the door to chaos.

Well, I swung the door wide open to chaos and gained an all-access pass to the universe. Some might consider this experience grounded in faith or truth; I just call it fact. Faith is knowing that something exists without any proof. Truth, on the other hand, is a mix of facts, faith, and illusion. A fact, however, is undeniable. And when a fact disrupts our truth, we either deny it or tango with chaos.

It's a fact that I can now talk to my mom and to other ghosts. I'm in constant touch with my guides and can see, smell, hear, and feel things that belong to the Other Side. I'm not saying that this whole process was easy, either. The old adage "no pain, no gain" is true. But pain and grief are part of life; they're a catalyst for growth. Brenda and my spiritual posse brought that point home and helped me perceive the world not in black and white but in Technicolor. Eventually the light made its way into darkness precisely *because* I had suspended my own disbelief and judgments and embraced chaos. I kept my heart and mind open and wrangled with the extraordinary. Once that all happened, I could really believe.

⌁

There are the stories in our lives that make us wonder how, when, and where we are all connected. Where do ideas come from? How and why do they come to us? I love the movie *Avatar* for the overall narrative premise that we're all connected: the energy of the trees, people, animals, water, and deceased loved ones.

Sometimes, in fact, we're connected in the oddest little ways. It's almost as if the universe has a sense of humor. This point comes home to me one day when, feeling like I was run over by a truck, I pay a visit Dr. Szeftel, my ear, nose, and throat specialist.

"Julie, I need you to lie down," Dr. Szeftel says.

I follow his order without question (which is proof right there that I'm really sick).

"Does your neck hurt?" he asks.

"No," I respond.

"Shoulders?"

"No."

"Bend your knee, please."

"What are you checking her for?" Suzanne pipes in.

"Viral meningitis. I've known her too long, Susan"—everyone screws up Suzanne's name—"and she's not right," he replies. Then he releases another round of rapid-fire questions and I respond to each:

Do you have any rashes? No.

Headaches? Yes.

Herpes? No.

Are you sleeping? Yes.

Back pain? No.

Have you been anyplace exotic? Yes, New Orleans.

"Well, I guess it could be that." Dr. Szeftel laughs with his deep New Zealand twang. "Could you go to work today and perform your duties?"

"No," I reply.

"Julie, could you have driven here today?"

"No."

Finally the doc gives us a diagnosis. "I think you have encephalitis. Suzanne, you need to take her home, keep an eye on her, don't let her do anything except watch television. No driving. No working for at least ten days." Then the good doctor prescribes antibiotics and sends us on our merry little way.

I have no idea what encephalitis is at the time, and perhaps you don't, either, so here it is in a nutshell: Encephalitis is inflammation of the brain. Yes, it's like a swollen brain. According to mayoclinic.org, the symptoms range from confusion, agitation or hallucinations, seizures, and loss of sensation in certain areas of the body, to muscle weakness, double vision, problems with speech or hearing, and loss of consciousness. Sounds lovely, doesn't it?

We have just entered into a New Year: 2015. I had decided to write this book on Christmas 2014 when my brain decided, ten days later, to go on hiatus in la-la land. La-la land is a scary place for a control freak like me, by the way.

I thought that menopause was bad, but I am wrong. I am really, really, really wrong.

I am slow. *Everything* is slow around me. I can't talk much, if at all. I look into the mirror and kinda recognize that person. I don't move much for five days after Dr. Szeftel's diagnosis. I burn a little sage and take a few shots with my iPhone in our backyard, but five minutes later I don't really remember doing it. There is certainly more activity happening outside of my brain then there is inside of it.

Monday rolls around and I delude myself into thinking that I'm ready to go back to work. (My mom instilled an intense work ethic in me from birth.) Still, I know that my body is nowhere ready to be back in the real world, much less my mind. I have to present our media campaign to our chairpeople at an 11 a.m. meeting and am petrified. I'm never petrified over these things. Give me the mic any day. But *today*? Who is this person who's afraid to speak?

I muddle through the presentation, barely alive. Later in the meeting I watch a bunch of new television commercials but can't keep up with them. For the rest of the day I barely exist. I try to recognize certain people and things. I also try to *avoid* certain people and things, particularly the stairs, as in: Remind me, please, how do I put one foot in front of the other without tumbling over myself in an involuntary cartwheel?

The next day doesn't feel terribly different. I don't want to eat or drink, either—another sure sign that I'm practically comatose. The only thing that briefly comes to mind is a Pop-Tart. I haven't had one in ten years (Pop-Tarts and weight loss don't make good bedfellows), but there it is: the vision of a sugary toaster pastry that's still a junk food favorite for millions of Americans.

I call Brenda and leave her a message. I had not talked with her since the previous week when she said she'd gotten hit hard with a bug that knocked her down for five days. Finally I'm sitting in my office when I get a call from her.

"Hello, my elf," she says.

"Oh thank God, witchy-poo. How are you?" I proceed to tell her everything about my doctor's visit and my weird-ass delirium.

"Uh-huh," Brenda says matter-of-factly, as if she knew exactly what I was going to say.

"Why did you respond with such familiarity?"

"That's what Dr. Dave tested me for: viral meningitis."

"No way. I didn't know you were having brain issues."

"I was out of it. Hardly raised my head for five days," Brenda says.

"Me, too." I give her more details about how shitty I've been feeling. "I wasn't in my body," I add. "A few times I actually thought that I might die. I thought this is what death was like. But I promised Suz that I'd be okay, so I fought to find something human, something relatable."

Brenda takes a deep breath, then says: "I think we had the same experience, except I just gave in to it. I was okay if I was dying. I thought I was dying, too."

"How funny that the essence of who we are came out during our temporary brain infection: I won't give in, it's just my nature. And you—you surrender. It's who you are. Neither is right or wrong. It's just who we are. Kinda cool, actually." After a beat I add: "Suz knew that something was wrong when I asked for Pop-Tarts."

There's a long pause on the other end of the line. Then: "What did you just say?"

"I said Suz should have clued in when—"

"The only time I spoke in five days is when David, my beloved, asked me if I was hungry, and I said that the only thing that sounded good was Pop-Tarts," Brenda replies.

There's another long pause, only now it's the sound of us both pondering in stunned silence the odds of this weird connection. I might be a sucker for Pop-Tarts, but Brenda? Processed foods are entirely off her radar. She eats kale, mung beans, ghee, and ayurvedic spices. A Pop-Tart is the last fucking thing that enters her culinary consciousness, let alone her pantry. Get the picture here?

Nothing psychic or spiritual ever shocks Brenda, but I think this Pop-Tart connection from the universe has pretty much done it.

I suddenly imagine Brenda and me hanging out in the astral plane while our physical bodies are wrestling with encephalitis.

"Hey," my astral self says. "Let's play a trick on our lower selves by repeating a code word that's totally out of the ordinary. What do you say, Brenda, you in?"

"Heck yeah," she replies. "How about Pop-Tarts? I've never eaten one in my life. And you're dieting right now, so odds are they're not in your food pantry. So that would be a sure sign for both of us."

Then we high-five in the astral plane and watch our sick physical bodies in different parts of the country lie around in bed, thinking about Pop-Tarts.

⤞⤝

Either way you view this experience, it certainly wasn't a coincidence. There's really no such thing. I call it divine timing. If everything is a coincidence, I'm pretty sure I wouldn't have experienced the wild side of the Other Side that shook me to my very core.

I now understand that everything is connected beyond our everyday comprehension. "I became aware that we're all connected," Anita Moorjani wrote in her bestseller *Dying to Be Me*. "This was not only every person and living creature, but the interwoven unification felt as though it were expanding outward to include *everything* in the universe—every human, animal, plant, insect, mountain, sea, inanimate object, and the cosmos. I realized that the entire universe is alive and infused with all of life and nature. Everything belongs to an infinite Whole. I was intricately, inseparably enmeshed with all of life. We're all facets of that unity—we're all One, and each of us has an effect on the collective Whole."

We all have to pay attention to who we are during the unpredicted and unscripted moments in our lives in order to experience our interconnectedness. We have to open ourselves up to the possibility that everything we assumed was impossible might in fact be possible. Only in those moments do we truly discover who we are.

*We all have to pay attention to who we are during*

*the unpredicted and unscripted moments in our*

*lives in order to experience our interconnectedness.*

*We have to open ourselves up to the possibility that*

*everything we assumed was impossible might in*

*fact be possible. Only in those moments do we truly*

*discover who we are.*

Are all those moments like a romp through the land of lolli-
pops? No, they are not. Sometimes they take you to a place where
you feel desperate and alone. The loss of my mom—and the mis-
taken belief that our connection was lost forever—catapulted me
onto this path of self-discovery. One of my favorite Brenda-isms
is this: "The universe gives you what you're supposed to have."
And you know what? It's not always sugar on a stick.

Sometimes we need to get knocked around a bit.

Or we need to experience pain and grief.

Sometimes our lives need to fall apart so we can rebuild them
from the foundation.

Or we need to experience rejection or the challenge of making a hard decision.

But when we're able to shed our self-pity, insecurities, or even
blame, we come to realize that even the devastating moments are
part of a greater path that will eventually lead us to an understanding of that interconnected whole that Moorjani refers to.

I now know that a soul connection can't be broken by the death
of a physical body. This, dear readers, falls into the indisputable
camp. I also know that unconditional love is just that: unconditional.

Still, I would love to say that I no longer fear death. I do—just not my own. The pain of losing someone you love is treacherous. But it can spark a flame that lights the path to an incredible learning experience not just about the universe, but about yourself. Every single day, through the ritual of prayer, grounding, and listening to my higher self, my light burns brighter, my path becomes more illuminated.

*A soul connection can't be broken by the death of a physical body. This, dear readers, falls into the indisputable camp. I also know that unconditional love is just that: unconditional.*

I'm so grateful to be able to communicate on a regular basis with my mom—the incredible woman who once refused a sangria—and my other guides like Jacob. These connections make my world quite peaceful and have changed me in so many ways, even small, unexpected ones. The other day I saved a damn bee from drowning in our pool; I watched the little fella buzz over the top of the water and land smack-dab in the middle of the pool. I balanced him on the back of my hand, then placed him on dry land where he shook the water off his wings, then flew away. Overall, I have to confess: I think I'm far more fucking delightful than I was before.

I also listen not just to spirits, but to humans, too. If you think you're having a one-on-one conversation with me, odds are it's a three-way conversation with Jacob chiming in when he feels it's helpful. In the past I was often so concerned about what I was going to say next that I'd forget to listen—or didn't particularly care to. Now, listening is instinctual and actually brings me more peace, because we all say dumb shit to fill a silent moment. If you're grounded and paying attention, dumb shit happens less frequently. And by the way, when I'm listening you might find me asking permission to share Jacob's insights with you. Taming my blurting ways was not easy, but it was incredibly pleasant for all involved.

If I had children, I'd tell them about my strange awakening. I'd tell them to remember that the ultimate superpower is indeed love. I'd tell them that by opening yourself to the possibility of impossibilities, you discover the magic within *and* the magic all around us, from the little black rock that you can hold in the palm of your hand for protection from unseen malevolent forces, to that voice you might hear from the Other Side that remarkably saves your life, to the swing of a pendulum that delivers a message from a higher energy (and let's not forget the alien that might show up in your backyard).

*If I had children, I'd tell them about my strange awakening. I'd tell them to remember that the ultimate superpower is indeed love.*

In the end, I'd tell my children to believe in our magical universe, even if at first glance it looks like make-believe.

# Protect Your Space: Brenda's Smudging and House-Clearing Instructions

## WHAT YOU WILL NEED

You'll need to acquire two sage smudge sticks and a candle or a good source of flame in case the stick goes out while you're working. Roll the stick between the palms of your hands a couple of times in order to loosen it a bit. If it's tied too tightly, it won't stay lit. Don't crush it, though, or it will burn too quickly.

You will also need something that you can use to fan the smoke of the smudge stick. I like to use a sacred feather tool but a hand fan or strong, thick paper or the back of a paper tablet will do, too. If you're using a paper product, it's always nice to decorate it or infuse with your energy or a picture of something that resonates with your spirit.

I also suggest you have a container that you can use to carry under the smudge stick while you're using it, as it will drop little bits of charred stick as you go. I like to use a large alabaster shell that is sacred to me, but any item you are comfortable with and that is noncombustible will do.

It's also nice to use a shell to have the element of the water to round out the elemental aspect—fire from the burning smudge stick, the air from the fanning, and the earth from the herbs.

## PREPARING FOR YOUR SMUDGING

I like to start at the "bottom" of the house and work my way up to the top level. So starting at the lowest level of the place you are about to clear, sit down on the floor, light your candle, and take three deep breaths, allowing your thoughts to clear and your inner/energetic body to expand more with each breath.

Say a prayer for protection—whatever you feel comfortable with that allows you to align with the divine, allowing nothing to come between that alignment. If you are familiar with your spirit guide, now would be a good time to call it in. If none of this sounds familiar or comfortable, then simply call in Archangel Michael, which is always a good move. Or you can use my favorite prayer for protection, which Brenda taught me:

> *I bring down a ray of divine light filled with love and protection and I draw a circle around my energetic body. Into the circle I place the white light of peace, the blue light of healing, the clear red light of energy, and the golden light of God. I direct that nothing and no one shall come between my circle and me. And so it is. Amen.*

## GETTING STARTED

Light your smudge stick from your candle. Let it burn about thirty seconds and then gently blow out the flame, like you could blow out a stick of incense, leaving a trail of smoke continuing to float up from the smudge stick.

Begin to "trace" the seams of each room with that trail of smoke. That means the floor-to-wall seam and the wall-to-wall seam (i.e., the ceiling to wall). You use the fanning tool throughout the whole process to send the smoke up each seam.

In addition to the seams of every room, you will also smudge the seams of windows, doorways (of rooms and closets), bookshelves, and mirrors. With your smudge stick or fan, make the infinity sign on each stair of the staircase and over mirrors and over drains (sinks, toilets, showers, bathtubs, washing machine, dishwasher) the same way. This symbol is particularly helpful in corners under furniture, or anyplace else energy feels "stuck."

After you complete each room, open a window or door to the outside and say the following phrase with authority and ownership, "Anything unaligned to my highest good, leave now!" Wait a minute or so, or until you feel the energy has cleared, and then close the window or door and move on to the next room or hallway.

After you complete every room, closet, hallway, and staircase you are done. Enjoy the freshness and lightness of your newly cleansed space. It's always nice to seal the process with a prayer of gratitude for the spirits who assisted you and then release them from this assignment.

If you're feeling as though you need to amplify your protection, you can always place a small trail of salt around the house or around the property. I also like to leave my smudging tools outside the front door as a symbol to any spirits even thinking about getting back in! Happy Smudging!

# Julie's Ghost Photography: Gallery of Ghosts

As I've mentioned earlier in these pages, discovering ghost photography was a seismic event, my personal inflection point. It marked my shift from psychic voyeur to psychic practitioner. That said, I've come to understand that not everyone sees what I do. Some people find the ghost photographs illusive; others are doubters and die-hard skeptics like I used to be.

Let's not dismiss the doubters.

Here's what I've heard from them:

"Ohhhh that's weird, but I don't see it."

"How do you know the smoke didn't make that pattern?"

"That looks like a Rorschach test."

"Maybe it's a shadow."

"That's not what I thought a ghost should look like."

Let me share my favorite conversation with one such skeptic. I was having lunch on a studio lot with a former boss. He's a giant among men, both physically and intellectually. We both share the graying of the mane and may be two of the only people I know who don't color their hair. He's too practical to color his hair. And me, well, I'm too damn lazy. The "natural look" is a bullshit excuse for being lazy. I use it regularly.

The only time I didn't wear T-shirts and jeans to work was many years ago when I had my first job interview with him. For that, I added a shirt that I bought at Old Navy for $3.50. During the interview he didn't ask much about my work experience; instead, he looked at the bottom of my résumé where it noted the full athletic scholarship for golf that got me into the University of Oklahoma. Our conversation went something like this:

"You play golf?"

"Yeah. I did."

"So you're a competitor?"

"Yeah."

"We need more of you."

I didn't turn him on with my slick connections to Hollywood royalty; I turned him on because I'm a competitor. He wanted fire, and that's what he got. He didn't bargain for ghosts, however.

Anyhow, one day years later I decided to test it out with him (my ghost photos, not my golf) when I saw him sitting in a booth in a commissary dining room. After giving him an uncomfortably (only to him) long hug, I sat down to enjoy an hour with the man who once said to me: "We can sleep when we're dead." This guy works harder than anyone in Hollywood. He is never satisfied and is intellectually curious. When he's not perfecting, he's studying—the ideal antagonist to my newly found metaphysical interests.

Our conversation went something like this:

*Him:* Jules. You look great. How's everything? I sure do miss you.
*Me:* I'm good, thanks. Been swimming every morning with my dog Homer, so I feel great. And I miss you, too.

After industry talk and gossip, we get to the good stuff.

*Him:* What else have you been up to?

*Me:* Well (*pause*), I mentioned in my e-mail that I wrote a
book.

*Him:* Yeah, what's it about?

*Me:* (*another pause*) It's called *The Ghost Photographer.*

He nods as if he knows what it's about.

*Me:* It's nonfiction.

*Him:* (*big laugh*) Well, you know, Jules, I don't believe in that
stuff.

*Me:* I know, and that's okay. You don't have to.

*Him:* Well, I know some people do; I just don't.

*Me:* Really, it's okay. I know this. The beauty of being you is
you get to choose. It's your truth.

The conversation continues as he catches me up about his
wife and kids. Fifteen minutes go by. Then . . .

*Him:* (*inquisitive look on his face*) Okay, so show me.

*Me:* (*little smirk on my face; I know exactly what he wants to
see*) Show you *what?*

*Him:* Your pictures.

I grab my iPad and first show him *The Pirate.*

*Him:* Ah, Jules, that looks like a Rorschach test.

I should have known better. Needed to up my game. So I
clicked on *Mr. Black Eye.*

*Me:* How about his one?

*Him:* Oh, I see that. He looks like a ghost for sure. But I still don't believe in ghosts.

*Me:* That's okay. Like I said, you don't have to if you don't want to. Your belief system, or your truth, doesn't align with the existence of ghosts. Mine didn't, either. So I understand.

*Him:* Let me see another one.

And so it went.

>━━✦

It really didn't matter that he didn't believe. We both walked away unscathed because we didn't try to dismantle each other's belief system. There isn't a photograph that could ever convince him of the existence of ghosts, just as there is no argument that could convince me that the physical world is all there is.

Let me repeat that: *There is no argument that could convince me that the physical world is all there is.*

>━━✦

So here's my truth: I see ghosts in my photographs. I *know* they're ghosts. I also know I've spent thousands of hours examining these photographs, and frankly, they are not what I thought ghosts were supposed to look like, either.

I hope you see what I see. It's magical for me. But I understand if they raise more questions or are simply unimpressive to you. They are here for you to decide.

Because I anticipate and welcome skepticism, I want to provide you with the original photos so you can see what I saw at first, and photos with pointers and descriptors after they've been highlighted with filters. (More on filters below.) These pics are in black and white, but you can go to www.julierieger.com to see them in their full-color glory.

Here are eight of my favorites:

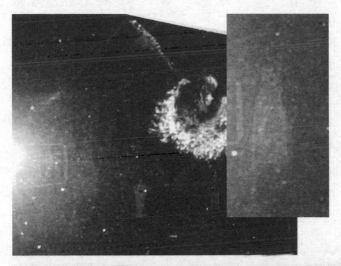

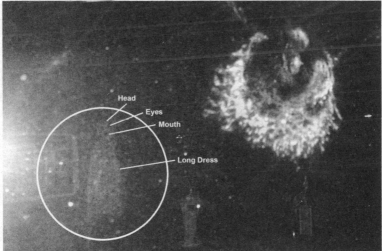

*This one started it all. I only saw the bird stain at first. Brenda opened my eyes to the lady on the left.*

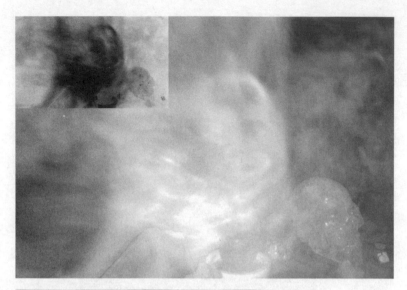

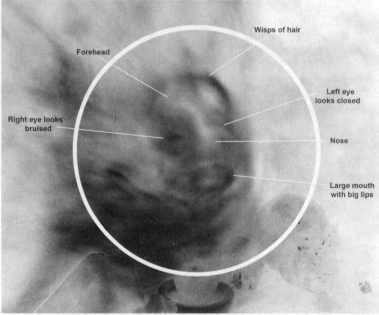

*This guy was hiding in a plume of sage smoke. He showed up about twice the size of a human head. I had to flip to negative mode to see his features. (More on what this means below.) I think he had a rough go while being a human.*

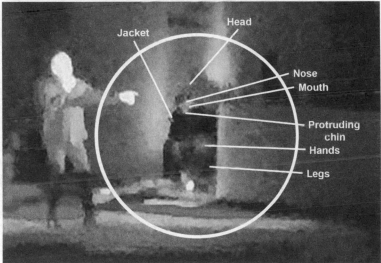

*I love Neil Diamond—and so did my mom—so I was giddy to go to his concert under the big half-shell dome of the Hollywood Bowl. I didn't think much of the photos I took until a few months later, when a friend liked one that I'd posted earlier on Facebook. I looked more carefully at the shot and there it was: someone or something in the corner of the stage that looks like a stagehand. I'm 100 percent positive that it was not there when I snapped the pic. How had I missed that? Once I adjusted the color scheme on the image I had a "holy shit" moment: The image did not change—this "person" was all one shade, which is a surefire sign of a ghost. I was positively delighted when I discovered this guy hanging out on the stage at the Hollywood Bowl.*

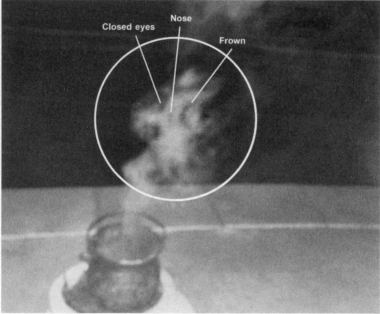

*You just look at her and feel her sadness. Why this Sad Lady ghost came to see me that night, I honestly do not know for sure. What I can tell you is that she's a reminder to live a happy life.*

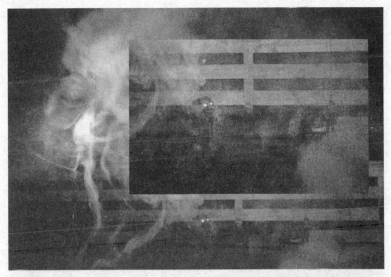

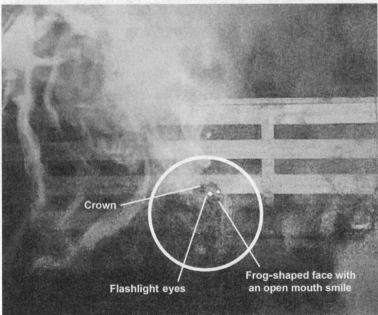

*Finding Kingfrog in this photo was a bit of an accident. I was searching through sage smoke when I saw him and his flashlight eyes next to the sage pot. His eyes are mesmerizing. Does he belong to the illustrious group that includes fairies and elves? Maybe.*

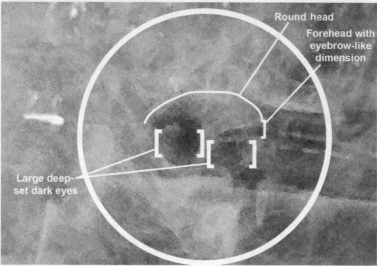

Round head

Forehead with eyebrow-like dimension

Large deep-set dark eyes

*Here is my peeping gray alien. On my website you'll notice that he actually is gray. I know that he's not terribly easy to see at first, but damn, when you do see him, he looks like every alien from every alien movie or graphic novel.*

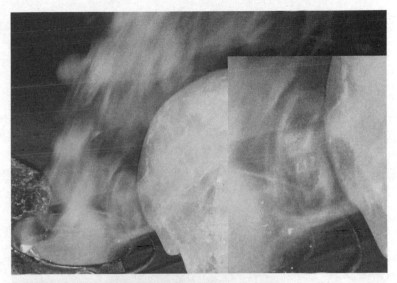

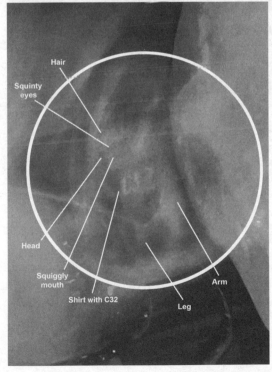

*I originally called C32 "Little Fucker" because I drove myself nuts trying to figure out what C32 meant. Out of all my ghost photographs, C32 is the most mysterious. It's also no taller than six or seven inches. I guess that makes it my mini and mysterious alien or ghost alien!*

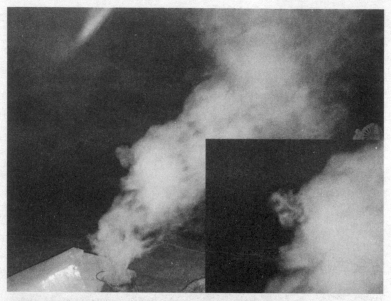

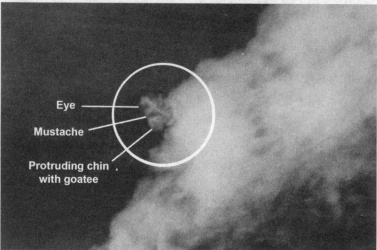

Eye

Mustache

Protruding chin
with goatee

*This guy looks like he belongs in a Popeye comic strip. He is one of countless different "heads" that poked out of a plume of smoke. I'd bet his head is roughly the size of a small dog. It's actually green in the original full-color photo on my website.*

# How to Catch a Ghost: Tips and Tricks

Here are some tricks of the trade to get you started if you're interested in pursuing ghost photography on your own.

In terms of equipment, I simply used my iPhone camera. I tried using a Samsung camera (not the phone camera) and all I got were orbs—little balls of light. If you're using an iPhone, turn off the HDR function, as it layers three pictures into one, which complicates and clutters your ghost photography. I've never used an Android phone, but give it a whirl; it might do the trick.

There are three areas I want to cover:

Naked photographs
Filtered photographs
"Smoke 'em out" photographs (as described in previous chapters)

## ABOUT CELL PHONE APPS

I use an app called PicShop that allows me to view my photographs through various filters. Each filter is like a lens that brings out depth and dimension that otherwise might not be apparent with the naked eye. Think of it this way: When you look at a bundle of clouds with your naked eye, you'll see a lot of white fluff in a sea of blue. Put on your sunglasses, however, and you'll suddenly see definition in the clouds: their outlines and various contours that actually differentiate each cloud from the other. You haven't modified the clouds; you've simply modified your vision in a way that lets you see them with more intensity and clarity.

Well, that's exactly what PicShop lets me—and you—do with photographs. And it's through this process that I was able to start discerning ghosts. So when I use the term "naked," I'm referring to my first "raw" photographs that haven't been filtered through PicShop.

## GETTING STARTED

When hunting for ghosts, always say a prayer of protection before you snap a single picture. As I've said throughout this book, protect your space and know the most important rule of all: *You are in charge of spirits that are not having a human experience.* Don't let them scare you.

## NAKED PHOTOGRAPHS

1. After you've taken your photographs, check every inch of the landscape of your shot to see if there is anything that shouldn't be there—or wasn't there when you took the shot.

2. Spirits often present themselves in light or in forms within light, so pay attention to this. (See *Kingfrog* in ap-

pendix two for an example.) When I first saw ghosts in my photos, I also saw colors that didn't belong in them, specifically purple and green. Fantasticals can present themselves in either one of these colors.

3. Ghosts often show up in mirrors, glass, or windows. You may find something peeking back at you.

4. Look for outlines in your photographs. This can be tough if you don't know what you're looking for, but persevere. Outlines are usually a shade darker or lighter than the background in which they appear. They can look like a paint-by-numbers drawing (before it's painted, of course).

5. If you question anything you see, zoom in—always zoom. Zooming is your friend.

Don't worry if you can't find any naked ghosts. We live in a world where we have the most powerful computing devices in the palm of our hand with applications for almost anything you can imagine. Photo apps like PicShop can help you find ghosts that are hiding in plain sight. Which brings us to our next step:

## FILTERED PHOTOGRAPHS

1. Upload your photo to PicShop and play around. Put your photo through various filters to look for shapes of fantasticals or spirits. Try the black-and-white function, then try different colored filters. Look carefully at each photo before moving on to a different filter. You can undo changes to get back to the original quite easily.

2. Take it a step further by using the "negative" filter. This is my favorite; no ghost can hide from the "negative" space. Depending on how light or dark your photo is, you may need an extra step of layering with the "spy" filter after you use the negative filter, which will give you additional contrast.

Once I find the ghosts, I sometimes change the colors after the "spy" stage, since some can be crisper than others. Just play around.

## SMOKE 'EM OUT

I accidently found ghosts by smoking them out when I thought I'd opened a ghost portal at our house (but ultimately didn't). I used sage smoke in an attempt to shoo them away, but the joke was on me, because it only made them more visible.

Should you choose to go down this path, please be careful, since you'll literally be playing with fire, and this can be incredibly dangerous. Take care of yourself, others, and your property. Always completely extinguish your sage or palo santo after your photo session. Use water to do this—you can't be too careful.

What you'll need: sage stick, heat-resistant pot or bowl (I prefer heavy metal or even enamel), lighter, and camera. And try to do this outside or everything in your home will smell like smoke.

1. Break apart your sage stick and place a handful in your bowl (depending upon size of bowl; use your good judgment).
2. Light the sage closest to the bottom of your burning pot or bowl. You may need a utility lighter (with a long

wand). Palo santo is a much friendlier indoor tool and the smell is divine. Follow the same instructions as you do with sage, sans the pot.

3. There will likely be flames for a minute or so. I like to take photos of the flames to see the images.

4. Once the flames are out, the smoke will begin to billow from your pot. Start snapping.

5. Sometimes I can take upward of a hundred photos in one session, so it takes me a long time to look at each one and decide which group I'd like to put through the photo app filter.

6. In addition to photo app filters, there are a few other filters I find handy for this type of ghost photo hunt.

   a) Under the "Edits" section of PicShop: brightness helps to either take it down or crank it up.

   b) Play with other filters in PicShop: "high color" shines a light on some ghosts; "red pop" or "dark pop" can help identify a ghost, too; "emboss" is interesting, as it gives your photo another dimension where you can see shapes.

   c) Always use the "negative" filter in addition to other filters. It's one of the most basic ways to see contrast in an image.

You may not always find a ghost, or you may not always see what someone else does. If you struggle with that, you can always e-mail me a photo or two and I'll try to uncover what may be hiding in your photo. Just submit your pics at www.julierieger.com.

# Daily Rituals and Spiritual Self-Care

Every culture has rituals. They connect us to our traditions, our sense of self, and more important, to a higher source. Some of us go to church, mosque, or temple for this. Others shy away from any organized form of ritual, seeking alternative ways to connect to something greater than themselves—or not. Either way, rituals are an inescapable part of life.

My daily spiritual rituals are fundamental for me. They're all about grounding myself and connecting to a higher source by moving and shifting energy around to prepare myself for the day ahead. That involves using visualization to move positive energy into my body, moving stale or negative energy out. Sometimes that energy I'm moving out comes from what happened the previous day—an interaction, emotion, or false idea about myself or others that might cause stress or anxiety. Other times, it's emotional stuff that's been sitting inside me for thirty years.

In other words, my daily ritual is a form of perpetual spiritual cleansing. Without it, I get tripped up by whatever triggers me: an asshole at work or an emotional fastball out of left field.

This grounding ritual is a variation of what Ima taught me, only instead of connecting me to the Other Side, it connects me to myself and to the Earth. In so doing, I spiritually align myself so I stay centered and act with grace and kindness throughout the day. You could simply say that it's a way to connect body and spirit. Without this connection, we're all a little like the title character in *Doctor Strange* when his astral self leaves his body. We get disconnected from self, which cultivates *dis*-ease. (And too much dis-ease can lead to disease—just sayin'.) I call my daily ritual the practice of grounding and allowing.

## VISUALIZATION

Most of us are familiar with the power of visualization. It's a meditative process that uses mental imagery to promote change in our lives. Some studies even suggest that physiologically we create neural pathways in our brains when we visualize things, as if we'd actually physically performed or experienced the action. (This explains, for example, why high-performing athletes use visualization on a regular basis.)

Visualization, in short, is a key part of my grounding ritual. Here's how I do it:

### Protecting

Every morning I sit in a chair or sofa with both feet firmly planted on the ground. The contact with my feet to the ground is important, because my feet chakras need to be connected to the Earth, which will later be part of my grounding process. I get quiet and move into a trancelike guided meditation, starting first with Brenda's prayer of protection.

## Grounding

Still quiet and with both feet on the ground, I close my eyes and visualize attaching a grounding cord to the back of my first chakra. Then I visualize sending this grounding cord down through all the rock and sediment under my feet, all the way to the center of the Earth. In my mind, it looks like a molten liquid concoction of yellows and reds, all swirling around and through one another. Once my cord hits this molten liquid, I visualize it being secured there.

This image is like having the security of an insurance policy: It's a strong visual prompt that I can summon throughout the day to stay grounded whenever anything throws me off: a person, an event, whatever it might be. It's like an anchor connected to the stable core of the Earth, because every day I go out into the world, and the world is full of fuckers and fastballs. Who doesn't need the extra protection? Of course, you can use whatever image you want: a cord, an anchor, a surfboard, an industrial chairlift pulley, a swizzle stick—you pick.

## Visualizing Golden Light

Once my grounding cord is intact, I now visualize golden light coming in through my seventh chakra, at the crown of my head. (See the list in appendix five, "The Crystal Kingdom," for a brief overview of chakras.) You can call this the Golden Light of God or the Golden Light of the Cosmic Muffin Top or whatever strikes your fancy. What's important is to visualize this golden light coming in through the crown of your head and traveling through your body as it clears out any negative or stuck energy from all of your organs and chakras. Slowly let everything turn gold within, visualizing that golden light going through your head and into your brain, eyes, nose, mouth, throat, shoulders, chest, and heart . . . all the way to the tips of your fingers and toes. Everything turns gold, including your skin (because don't forget: your skin is an organ).

Gold, by the way, is the color of illumination, enlightenment, wisdom, and deep insights into the heart and soul. Countless books dive deep into the incredible universe of colors, which are associated with so many important attributes: love, strength, power, serenity, purity—the list goes on. Colors can soothe or irritate; raise or lower blood pressure. I encourage you to explore the world of color on your own.

I have an intimate connection to certain colors that give me information during my rituals. Pink, the color of love, is always an indication that I need to lead with my heart; purple, the color of royalty, is a sign that I'm going to encounter "royals" in my life. For the purpose of this exercise, let's stick with the glory of gold.

Once you've visualized this powerful color traveling throughout your body, you have effectively purified and fortified yourself. This exercise is as essential to me as my daily swims with Homer that set the groundwork for the entire day. And these effective rituals can support you, too, every day of your life.

## NIGHTTIME RITUAL

Of course day turns into night, and night brings with it the restorative power of sleep. Since morning and evening are spiritual bookends to my day, I always practice a night ritual. Before I go to bed (dressed in my favorite Kermit-the-Frog-playing-the-banjo sleep shorts and tank top), I light a stick of sacred palo santo wood. Once the smoke begins to billow from the tip of the stick, I walk in a clockwise circle around the bedroom saying this alternative version of Brenda's prayer of protection:

*I bring down a ray of divine light, filled with love and protection. I draw a circle around the energetic body of my family. Into the circle I place the white light of peace, the blue light of healing, the clear red light of energy, and the golden light of God. And I direct that nothing or no one shall come between my family and its circle. So it is. Amen.*

I move clockwise because, to recap, moving clockwise brings energy *in*; moving counterclockwise moves energy *out*.

While the palo santo is still lit, I pray. I thank God for giving me another day. I thank the angels for protecting me. I thank Jacob for guiding me. I thank my ancestors for watching over me. And I thank my mother and father for giving me life and teaching me unconditional love. Then I snuff out the palo santo in a brass bowl on my nightstand that sits next to a large chunk of double terminated black tourmaline.

Now guess what? When I wake up, I do it all over again.

My practice is to live in gratitude each day. It doesn't always happen that way, though, I have to confess. Just like everyone else, I can be thrown off my center. I can lash out in anger. I can be pathetic. I can be needy. I can be arrogant. I can be selfish. I call it my practice because I literally practice each day for those egocentric moments to be fewer and more far between. I practice each day to speak my truth without fear of consequence or approval. I practice each day to be kind even if the other person in my face is an asshole. I practice each day to be nonjudgmental. (I guess I should retract the previous asshole comment.)

What matters is that I have a ritual, a practice. Like with anything else—any sport, art, or trade—we must practice to be better.

# The Crystal Kingdom: Five Crystals That Every Human Must Have

I hold a crystal in my hand every time I practice my daily rituals. Usually it's a rose quartz, but as you know by now, many crystals are an integral part of my life. I love all the crystals in the crystal kingdom and could wax on for another few more hundred pages—but I'll cut to the chase: If I had to pick only five crystals that every human should have, here's my must-have list:

## 1. BLACK TOURMALINE

It's no surprise that if I had to choose only one crystal for the rest of my life, it would be black tourmaline. It's my king stone. When I'm taking ghost photographs or house clearing, you can bet I've got black tourmaline in all my pockets. I also have a plastic bucket in my backseat floorboard filled with black tourmaline. (You've never heard of anyone who had a car accident with a bucket of black tourmaline in their car, have you?) I have pieces in luggage, in my pocket, in my handbag, on my desk at work and home, and on every windowsill in the house. Its energy protects and strengthens me, and also helps me sleep well. It should be on every single bedside table in every single bedroom.

## 2. AMETHYST

Amethyst crystals are all a variation on the powerful color purple. They're associated with serenity and are imbued with a high level of spiritual energy. Similar to black tourmaline, amethyst finds a place on my bedside table to help me sleep well and in various rooms where I work, where it promotes calm, radiant energy.

## 3. ROSE QUARTZ

Hold rose quartz in your hand and close your eyes, and you can just feel love. Its pink color is associated with our fourth chakra, the heart chakra. Rose quartz represents unconditional love, compassion, peace, and comfort; it clears out anger, resentment, and bitterness.

## 4. CITRINE

Citrine relates to earthly matters of survival and power—and essential resources like money—all of which are connected to our sense of self-worth. Its radiant yellow and gold color energizes and activates the third chakra of our solar plexus, which relates to our digestive tract and central nervous system.

## 5. CLEAR QUARTZ CRYSTAL

If there's any stone that embodies almost every attribute in the crystal kingdom, it's clear quartz crystal. It's known as the "master healer" of all crystals and evokes the transparent power of water. People use it to heal various parts the body, neutralize negative energy, and harmonize all the chakras.

## CHAKRAS

For your reference, here's a quick look at each chakra: its name, location, color, associated organs, and energy. There are thousands of books available for anyone interested in learning more about chakras.

### CHAKRA QUICK REFERENCE CHART

| NUMBER | NAME | LOCATION | COLOR | ORGANS | ENERGY |
|--------|------|----------|-------|--------|--------|
| First | root | base of spine | red | spine, limbs, circulatory system | survival |
| Second | sacral | below belly button | orange | reproductive organs, kidneys, bowels, immune system | emotions |
| Third | solar plexus | upper abdomen | yellow | pancreas, liver, digestive tract, skin, central nervous system | self-worth |
| Fourth | heart | center of chest | *lower:* pink; *upper:* green | thymus, heart, lower lungs, circulatory system, immune system | love |
| Fifth | throat | throat | blue | thyroid, respiratory system, teeth, vocal cords | communication and self-expression |
| Sixth | third eye | between the eyes | indigo | pituitary, eyes, sinuses | intuition and wisdom |
| Seventh | crown | top of the head | violet | pineal gland, brain, nervous system | connection to spirituality |

# Gratitude

I don't know how to begin to thank everyone named in this book. To me, you're not just a name, you are what makes me, me.

These experiences I describe in this book are part of us, part of our lives. And I believe that they are also bigger than us: They're proof, whether in the form of photography or personal experience, that we are indeed spirits having a human experience. I didn't understand this until you came into my life.

I thank you all for not making me feel crazy and for supporting me in my journey. I thank you for being by my side through tremendous grief, and for helping me find joy again. I thank you for listening to my stories—what seemed to be unbelievable—of the unseen world. And thank you for telling me yours.

To Suzanne: What a privilege it is to be your wife, your partner in this life. Thank you for picking me not only when it was easy, but, more important, when it was hard. Thank you for never telling me that. You keep me grounded. You make me better. Wherever you are is home. It is an honor to grow old with you. I have loved you for many lifetimes, I feel sure.

To Brenda: Because of you, I believe in magic. If not for your wisdom, open heart, extraordinary gifts, and unwavering friendship, I would be twirling with no true north. It is an honor to be your elf. You have my love and devotion for eternity.

To Mona: I miss you every single day. I drive by your house on my way to work and my heart sinks without fail. In life you taught me warmth and devotion, and I taught you that you can't make French toast in a toaster. In death, I learned that you were still here. Honestly, with your son in our house, it was hard to ignore you. Our electronics worked perfectly after he moved out. I love you, Mona. I will see you again.

To Pam (Mona's sister): Thank you for grieving with me, for understanding my inconsolable pain. Thank you for being the funniest sad person on the planet. I am so sorry that you lost so much that horrible night on the way back to LA from Lake Havasu. I know you will never be the same. I admire your courage, your devotion to your husband and to your sister. You love so very deeply it's a curse and a gift. I will always love you so very much.

To Patricia: I love everything about you, from your prickly exterior to your marshmallow heart. I thank you for teaching me to trust my intuition and to believe in my own powers. I thank you for teaching me about the power of crystals. You are one badass psychic lady who is very picky about her friends; I am honored to be one of them. I can honestly say that I have loved every single second I have spent with you so far on this Earth. That's hard to find.

To Ima: I don't know how to properly thank you. Here it goes: Thank you for including me in your psychic tribe. You shared not only your gifts with me, but an extraordinary amount of time, which is one of our most precious resources. I am most grateful for this gift from you. Instead of handing me a fish, you taught me how to be a kickass fisherman.

To Tony Sella: My friend, my former boss, my brother from another lifetime, I love you. You are my mirror. Through you I see who I am on so many levels and dimensions. I know your kindness, your genius, and your beautiful crazy. You will forever by my teacher of the creative gifts from the universe.

To Cubby, my sister from another mother: We know everything about each other. You are my rock, my keeper. I have never once felt alone on this Earth because of you. I will love you until the end of time.

To Julie Piepenkotter: I thank you for being my smart friend who knows how to spell and use proper punctuation. I swear on my life that autocorrect just kicked in when I tried to spell punctuation. Aside from your incredible grasp of the English language, you are my friend with a giant heart who was so willing to read and read and read and talk and talk and talk about this book. We learned so much about each other through the process and this body of work, which is better as a result of you. You made me find more of me.

To my friends Sari and Becca: I keep you two apart for a reason; together you would torture me relentlessly. Separately, you have stuck by me day in and day out, encouraging me to dig deeper and on occasion be funnier when I was exhausted by life. I love you both.

To my friend and master of the advertising universe JoAnn Ross: It was you. It was you who encouraged me to move fearlessly and share my story with Carolyn Reidy. Our bond is not what we do for a living, but our unwavering love for our moms. I will forever be grateful to you, JoAnn.

And to you, Carolyn Reidy, and you, Judith Curr: My God did you take a chance with me. I admire your faith and commitment to finding new voices in the strangest places. I would certainly call ghost photography a strange place. I would also say, as a businesswoman, that you are both leaders who inspire other women (don't worry, we're watching you). No guts, no glory, right? I will forever be grateful to you and for picking Zhena to guide me down this path I never traveled.

To my publisher, Zhena Muzyka: Everything about you is magical, from your own writings, your storytelling, your love, and your family, to your compassion for every single living thing. There was no publisher in the world better for me than you. Thank you for loving my voice when I didn't even know I had one. And thank you for knowing me before I knew myself. Your vision will heal others. Your soul is so giant, I don't know how it fits in that little body of yours. I will follow you anywhere.

To my editor and ghostwriter, Debra Ollivier: You are not just an editor or a ghostwriter to me, you're now a friend, a member of my tribe. You taught me proper storytelling. You pushed me to reveal the depths of my soul to better serve our readers. And the funny thing is this, it served me, too. You're like a coach who also plays in the game. Thank you for being my coach and for opening your home and your life to me. I hope this is just our beginning. To you, I give you my devotion and admiration.

To Stacey Snider: I have worked for and with many great women in my life, but not one like you. You exude class, utter brilliance, genuine kindness, self-deprecation, and a wicked sense of humor. And you're tough as fucking nails. You blazed a trail for not only women like me, but women everywhere. We are indebted to you. Your husband had it right when he said you're a combination of Lucy Ricardo and Albert Einstein. Working for you is enchanting.

To a real hero and psychic soul sister, my photo editor, Ariell Brown: Sister, you are the first person I have encountered who sees everything that I do. Only you could usher my ghosts into the light where everyone else can see them.

To my dog, Homer: In the moments when I was petrified that I opened a ghost portal, you were right there by my side. We would walk the perimeter of the property together, burning sage, praying, and talking to your grandma Margaret asking her to protect our family and home. You are the first dog I ever truly loved. I am you in a human suit. We both bark a lot, we both love a good snack, we both sense danger, we both don't come when our name is called, we both know Booger is in charge of the house, but most important, we are fiercely loyal to each other and those we love.